MORE THAN A FEELING

WORSHIP THAT PLEASES GOD

Dear Brad,

I would like to pass this book along to you. Please dont feel I am judging you. I would read this book but music is not one of my strengths and giftedness.

Gary A. Knoblauch

P.S. after reading this book please pass it along to ~~Scott~~. Scott Deckert

MORE THAN A FEELING

WORSHIP THAT PLEASES GOD

JIMMY JIVIDEN

GOSPEL ADVOCATE COMPANY
P.O. BOX 150
NASHVILLE, TENNESSEE 37202

Published by Gospel Advocate Co.
P.O. Box 150, Nashville, TN 37202
http://www.gospeladvocate.com

ISBN 0-89225-381-9

With deep appreciation I dedicate this book to my wife, Shirley; my children, Steve and Marta Jividen; Diane and Dale Huff; and Debbie and James McCoy.

ACKNOWLEDGEMENTS

Every author knows that his work is not solely his own. It is rather the product of truths learned and influences felt by innumerable people who have touched his life. This certainly holds true for this book. Long time friends, esteemed preachers, eminent scholars and my personal family have read and critiqued my work to make it more accurate and readable.

This includes Tim and Linda Appleton, Jack Grant, Dale Huff, Cecil May, Howard Norton, Bill Proctor, Phil Sanders and Greg Tidwell. My wife, Shirley, meticulously proofed the manuscript during its preparation; Jack Lewis offered wise and scholarly counsel. Linda Appleton sought to correct my grammar and style. Others offered suggestions for content and form. The Oldham Lane church with whom I serve was supportive, and my publisher took care of the innumerable details in the publishing process.

TABLE OF CONTENTS

PREFACE

Jesus' disciples asked Him, "Teach us to pray." They were concerned about their worship. Jesus responded to their quest by both teaching and modeling prayer. His disciples nearly 2,000 years later still need to learn more about worship and worshiping. This book seeks to meet this need. It might be called a "workbook on worship."

It seeks to be non-technical and practical, adapted to Bible class and personal study. Its 13 chapters have discussion questions at the end of each chapter and practical recommendations for improving worship in the Christian assembly.

For a more detailed study on the nature and practice of worship in the New Testament, see Everett Ferguson, *The Church of Christ* published by Eerdmans in 1996, pages 207-277. For a more detailed study on worship by singing, see my book, *Worship in Song*, published by Star in 1987.

The purpose of this book is to affirm the New Testament practice of worship. The reasons for rejecting some of the current worship innovations and abuses will become clear by this affirmation. This book is designed to stimulate discussion. Worship changes or non-changes should not be made for sociological, generational or political reasons, but from a study of the Scriptures.

This book will be read by worship leaders but is focused on the needs of people in the pew. Study questions are at the end of the chapters. There are no footnotes or personal polemics. Practical suggestions are given that may help in learning about and improving worship in the church.

All Scripture texts, unless otherwise indicated, come from the New American Standard Bible.

THE NATURE
OF WORSHIP

The study of any subject should begin with the definition of terms. There are great gulfs between the different interpretations of the word "worship." If one person understands worship to mean one thing and another regards it as something entirely different, it will be difficult for them to have a meaningful discussion.

One person might understand worship to mean an attitude while another might understand it to be an act. A third person might understand that it involves both. All may use the term, but be in radical disagreement over the content of its meaning.

Some may view worship as so vague that it defies definition. Others may view worship so subjectively that it can mean anything one wants it to mean. Still others will understand worship to mean the way it is described in the Scriptures. Such diverse views of the meaning of worship make discussion difficult.

Section 1 deals with the nature of worship. It attempts to define, describe and limit the meaning of worship to what is revealed in the biblical text.

CHAPTER ONE

WHY DO
WE WORSHIP?

John 4:19-24; Acts 14:15-17; 17:22-31;
Romans 1:18-22

It is our very nature to worship. We were created that way. Angels worship (Hebrews 1:6). All people will worship God at the Judgment (Philippians 2:10). The heavenly host with the redeemed of the ages will worship God in heaven throughout eternity (Revelation 14:1-3). The practice of worship begun on earth will continue in heaven.

THE WONDER OF EXISTENCE

Regardless of our culture or age, we wonder about our existence, our nature and our destiny. We can observe creation but know we are not the Creator. We do not control the world around us but marvel at the laws which do. We instinctively know that the world's existence and the laws which control it did not come from nothing. Reason demands an unknown first cause. Worship is a way we seek to contact and understand this "hidden void" of reason. No doubt this awareness motivated David to write, "The heavens are telling of the glory of God; And their expanse is declaring the work of His hands" (Psalm 19:1).

An emptiness exists in the psyche of each of us. We are composed of matter like the world in which we live and have life like the animals we observe in nature. A certain dimension of our being, however, is different. We can reason, will and love. We are spirits. This spiritual nature longs to commune with God who is spirit. A God-shaped void exists in all of us.

These attributes along with our feelings of smallness in and ignorance of the universe make us wonder why things are like they are. There must be an explanation beyond this time-bound physical universe. This wonder makes us grope for God. We seek to know Him who is all-powerful, all-knowing and unlimited by time and matter. Such a quest is not in vain. God has revealed Himself both in nature and in revelation. Paul affirmed this: "For since the creation of the world His invisible attributes, His eternal power and divine nature, have been clearly seen, being understood through what has been made, so that they are without excuse" (Romans 1:20).

Within each of us dwells an urge to know our Creator, who controls creation and holds the future in His hands. Without God's revelation of Himself, we grope in darkness and ignorance. Paul noted this knowledge in speaking to the philosophers at Athens:

> He Himself gives to all people life and breath and all things; and He made from one man every nation of mankind to live on all the face of the earth, having determined their appointed times, and the boundaries of their habitation, that they would seek God, if perhaps they might grope for Him and find Him (Acts 17:25-27).

We are spiritual beings and seek fellowship with God who is Spirit. We live among God's other created things and depend on them for livelihood, but a loneliness within us seeks for communion with the good and giving God.

Worship is a universal experience in every culture. The idols around the Parthenon at Athens were not the only objects of pagan devotion. Some people worshiped the sun. Some worshiped ancestors. Some worshiped the emperor. Some worshiped fertility. Idols were found on hills, by rivers, in groves, in marketplaces, in surrounding government buildings and in most houses.

People made idols, but the idols had no life. People stimulated excitement in the mystery religions, but it was merely manipulated emotional feelings. People formulated rituals to woo the favor of God but found them to be self-serving and self-deluding. People's quest for God on their own terms has been fruitless, but God has not left Himself without witness. Paul told the pagan worshipers at Lystra about such a God: "He did not leave Himself without witness, in that He did good and gave you rains from heaven and fruitful seasons, satisfying your hearts with food and gladness" (Acts 14:17).

David knew the true and living God, the eternal and all powerful Creator God, the good and giving God who desires to be worshiped. He sang of his desire to be in His presence: "As the deer pants for the water brooks, so my soul pants for Thee, O God. My soul thirsts for God, for the living God" (Psalm 42:1-2). Psalm 23 reflects the sweet communion and trusting confidence David knew because of his spiritual relationship with God:

> The Lord is my shepherd, I shall not want.
> He makes me lie down in green pastures;
> He leads me beside quiet waters.
> He restores my soul;
> He guides me in the paths of righteousness
> For His name's sake.
> Even though I walk through the valley of the
>   shadow of death,
> I fear no evil, for Thou art with me.
>
> (Psalm 23:1-4)

THE WONDER OF ORIGINS

Even Greek philosophers ventured on a quest for God. The philosophers sought the "first cause," which they regarded as a rational necessity. Aristotle reasoned back to the "Unmoved Mover" and Plato to the "Form of the Good." These postulated "first causes" were not personalized into divine beings, but generated questions that could only find a satisfactory answer in God. Anselm later used this process to show the rational necessity of God. The existence and worship of the Creator is the logical common sense conclusion of His orderly creation and the principle of "cause and effect."

In contrast to the Greek philosophical speculations about the first cause stands the prophetic affirmation of the power and majesty of the only true and living God:

> Who has measured the waters in the hollow of
>   His hand,
> And marked off the heavens by the span,
> And calculated the dust of the earth by measure,
> And weighed the mountains in a balance
> And the hills in a pair of scales? ...
> Behold, the nations are like a drop from a bucket,
> And are regarded as a speck of dust on the
>   scales; ...
> All the nations are as nothing before Him,
> They are regarded by Him as less than nothing
>   and meaningless. ...
> "To whom then will you liken Me That I should be
>   his equal?" says the Holy One.
>   (Isaiah 40:12, 15, 17, 25)

THE WONDER WITHIN US

Whether it is Allah, Buddha, ancestors or idols, every culture has objects of ultimate concern that are worshiped. Worship is the natural thing to do. A thinking person who contemplates his existence, origin and nature must stand in awe of that nature and the surrounding universe. David expressed this awe in one of his songs:

> For Thou didst form my inward parts;
> Thou didst weave me in my mother's womb.
> I will give thanks to Thee, for I am fearfully and
>   wonderfully made;

Wonderful are Thy works,
And my soul knows it very well.

(Psalm 139:13-14)

Two classic studies of the religious experiences of individuals from a psychological point of view are William James' book, *The Varieties of Religious Experience*, published in 1902, and Rudolph Otto's book, *The Idea of the Holy*, published in 1917. Both reflect the universal need for worship.

James defined religion and the response to divinity this way:

... [T]he feeling, acts and experiences of individual men in their solitude, so far as they apprehend themselves to stand in relation to whatever they may consider the divine (p. 42).

... The divine shall mean for us only such a primal reality as the individual feels impelled to respond to solemnly and gravely, and neither by a curse nor a jest (p. 47).

Otto discussed this universal religious experience related to worship, coining the words "*numinous*," "*mysterium tremendum*" and "*Wholly Other*" in seeking to explain the universal psychological experience of religion. He considered the numinous as the unique object of religious apprehension, beyond reason, the good and the beautiful. "*Numinous*" was coined from the Latin *numen*, which Otto used to stand for "[a] unique original feeling-response, which can be in itself ethically neutral and claims consideration in its own right" (p. 20).

"*Mysterium tremendum*" refers to an experiential state related to worship. Otto described it like this:

[T]he feeling of it may at times come sweeping like a gentle tide, pervading the mind with a tranquil mood of deepest worship. It may pass over into a more set and lasting attitude of the soul, continuing, as it were, thrillingly vibrant and resonant, until at last it dies away and the soul resumes its profane, non-religious mood of everyday experience. It may burst in sudden erup-

tion up from the depths of the soul with spasms and con-
vulsions, or lead to strangest excitements, to intoxicat-
ed frenzy, to transport, and to ecstasy. ... Conceptually
mysterium denotes merely that which is hidden and es-
oteric, that which is beyond conception or understanding, extraordinary and unfamiliar (pp. 26-27).

Tremendum involves fear, but wholly distinct from that of being afraid. It suggests awe and religious dread.

Otto employed the term "*Wholly Other*" to describe the concept of divinity from a psychological point of view. Otto described
it this way:

Taken in the religious sense, that which is mysterious
is ... The *Wholly Other*. ... That which is quite beyond
the sphere of the usual, the intelligible, and the familiar, which therefore falls quite outside the limits of the
"canny" and is contrasted with it, filling the mind with
blank wonder and astonishment (p. 40).

Our very nature cries out for God. Our spiritual existence is
an empty void without God. Our rational mind cannot find a first
cause without God. Our psyche has feelings beyond understanding without God. Only through acknowledging and worshiping God can we fulfill the natural yearnings of our spirit.
There is no escaping the presence of God; He is everywhere.
The psalmist wrote:

Where can I go from Thy Spirit?
Or where can I flee from Thy presence?
If I ascend to heaven, Thou art there;
If I make my bed in Sheol, behold, Thou art there.
If I take the wings of the dawn,
If I dwell in the remotest part of the sea,
Even there Thy hand will lead me,
And Thy right hand will lay hold of me.
(Psalm 139:7-10)

THE NEGLECT OF TRUE WORSHIP

Worship is a universal experience not confined to those who follow the God of the Bible. It is a part of the very nature of every person. In every person exists an emptiness that only God can fill. People who do not fill this void with devotion to the true God will fill it with delusions, which explains the origin and practice of idolatry. Paul noted the four steps leading away from the true worship of God into pagan idolatry:

> For even though they knew God, they did not honor Him as God or give thanks, but they became futile in their speculations, and their foolish heart was darkened. Professing to be wise, they became fools, and exchanged the glory of the incorruptible God for an image in the form of corruptible man and of birds and four-footed animals and crawling creatures (Romans 1:21-23).

First came neglect of the worship of the true God. Second, this neglect led to foolish speculation arising from their own deluded minds. Third, these speculations took on forms of all kinds of idolatry. Fourth, God gave them over to impure lusts, degrading passions and a depraved mind.

Such a process accounts for the foolish, irrational and even evil things done in the name of religion. The neglect of true worship leads to the error of perversions and the triumph of evil. Neglecting worship leads to spiritual suicide.

Note that the speculation of deluded minds and the practice of all kinds of idolatry finally resulting in gross immorality were first initiated by the neglect of true worship of the only God. The practice of worship, its nature and its form are all central to religion. It can almost be said, "As a person worships, so is he."

Although the desire for worship dwells in the heart of every person, the devil seeks to compromise and pervert it with his lies. This is shown in one of the temptations of Jesus:

> Again, the devil took Him to a very high mountain and showed Him all the kingdoms of the world and their glory; and he said to Him, "All these things will I give

You, if You fall down and worship me." Then Jesus said
to him, "Begone, Satan! For it is written, 'You shall worship the Lord your God, and serve Him only' "
(Matthew 4:8-10).

Jesus quoted from Deuteronomy 6:13 in His response to the
devil. The word for "only" is not in any of the most ancient man-
uscripts of the Hebrew text and is left out or italicized in most
English translations. Jesus followed the Septuagint by adding
"only" (*autoi monoi*).

Jesus' response to the devil showed that He understood the silence of Scripture to be prohibitive. The Scriptures did not say,
"Thou shalt not worship the devil." They affirmed who was to be
worshiped, excluding all others. Moses did not have to name all
of the false gods man was not to worship. In his affirmation of who
was to be worshiped, all others were excluded. This still is the way
to resist false worship. We must not be involved in worship practices or give homage to objects that have no Scriptural authority.
Jesus quoted the word of God to show what was acceptable worship. This excluded all things that "God commanded not."

The devil is the author of perverted worship. He makes it appear attractive and rewarding. Jesus rejected the dishonest offer
made by the devil because it lacked the authorization of Scripture.

QUESTIONS

1. Describe the feeling of a God-shaped void that is in every man.
2. Name the steps leading to idolatry in Romans 1:21ff and discuss how they might instruct us today in our worship.
3. Does it make any difference who and in what way we worship?
   Give Scriptural examples.
4. Identify some circumstances in which you experience the
   "need" to worship.
5. What happens to spiritual growth when worship is neglected?
   Give examples.
6. Check the Old Testament source of the passage Jesus quoted
   to the devil in Deuteronomy 6:13. What did Jesus add to the
   quotation and why?

CHAPTER TWO

WHAT IT MEANS TO WORSHIP

Matthew 4:8-10; John 4:19-24; 1 Corinthians 12-14

Jesus had just finished praying when one of His disciples asked, "Lord, teach us to pray just as John also taught his disciples" (Luke 11:1). His followers wanted to learn how to worship in prayer. They understood that worship is active. It is not something that happens to you; it is something you do. It is more than a psychological response to religious rituals performed by others; it is an individual spiritual communion with the high and holy God. Worship can be both taught and learned.

WORSHIP WORDS

To understand what it means to worship, we must understand the terms used for worship in the New Testament. There are ten Greek terms which are translated "worship." Three of the terms appear only once. Nine of the terms combine with the Greek term *seb* and mean "to venerate." *Leitourgeo* appears five times and refers to the "spiritual service" of sending benevolent contributions or participating in a preaching-teaching ministry. The two most used and most descriptive terms translated "worship" in the New Testament are *proskuneo* (59 times) and *latreuo* (18 times). *Proskuneo* focuses more on the attitude of the worshiper, and *latreuo* focuses more on the act of worship itself.

Proskuneo is defined as:

> the custom of prostrating oneself before a person and kissing his feet, the hem of his garment, the ground etc., the Persians did this in the presence of their deified king, and the Greeks before a divinity or something Holy" (Arndt, Gingrich and Danker, p. 723).

Latreuo is defined as:

> serve, in our lit. Only of carrying out of relig. duties, esp. of cultic nature, by human beings (Arndt and Gingrich, p. 468).

> It is not enough to say that *latreuein* has religious significance. One must say that it has sacral significance. *Latreuein* means more precisely to serve or worship cultically, especially by sacrifice (*G. Kittel's Theological Dictionary of The New Testament*, Vol. IV, p. 60).

Worship on the one hand involves the inner attitude of the worshiper (*proskuneo*) and on the other hand the external acts he does in worship (*latreuo*). They must not be separated. Jesus used both words in His response to the temptation of the devil: "You shall worship [*proskuneo*] the Lord your God, and serve [*latreuo*] Him only" (Matthew 4:10). *Proskuneo* describes an attitude which excludes "word-only worship," and *latreuo* excludes the perversion of unauthorized acts.

In Spirit and Truth

Jesus' conversation with the Samaritan woman was about both the attitude and the act of worship:

> The woman said to Him, "Sir, I perceive that You are a prophet. Our fathers worshiped in this mountain, and you people say that in Jerusalem is the place where

men ought to worship." Jesus said to her, "Woman, believe Me, an hour is coming when neither in this mountain, nor in Jerusalem, shall you worship the Father. You worship that which you do not know; we worship that which we know, for salvation is from the Jews. But an hour is coming, and now is, when the true worshipers shall worship the Father in spirit and truth; for such people the Father seeks to be His worshipers. God is spirit, and those who worship Him must worship in spirit and truth" (John 4:19-24).

This passage reflects four important facts about worship.

First, Christian worship is not confined to a physical place. The Samaritans worshiped on Mount Gerizim and the Jews on Mount Zion. Jesus showed that the internal spirit of a person is the locus of worship, not some external holy place on a mountain.

Second, the Father desires worship from His people. Jesus said, "Such people the Father seeks to be His worshipers." God is not some stoic, non-caring, impassive deity. He wants to commune with His people in worship.

Third, it does make a difference whether we follow God's directions in worship. Jesus corrected the Samaritan woman's misconception on where God wanted His people to come to worship. It was Jerusalem, not Gerizim. He said, "You worship that which you do not know; we worship that which we know; for salvation is from the Jews." Although this would become a moot point with the coming of Christ's kingdom, Jesus thought it necessary to stress that worship is to be done the way God directs, not according to the way humans devise.

Fourth, we must worship in spirit and truth. People interpret the word "spirit" a number of ways. Some suggest that the term refers to the "spiritedness" with which worship is expressed – excitement. Others suggest that "spirit" involves inspired utterances given by God – a miracle. These interpretations are foreign to John 4 as well as to the other New Testament teachings about the nature of worship. Worshiping "in spirit" refers to the spiritual communion which takes place when our spirit joins with God, who is Spirit. Our spirit transcends the physical, temporal and mortal limits of humanity and worships God in the spiritual realm.

"Truth" may refer to the God-authorized acts revealed in Scripture. Certainly worship must be scriptural. Jesus said, "Thy word is truth" (John 17:17). It may also mean that worship must be genuine, not counterfeit. Certainly worship must be "truthful." Worship is "vain" that does not come from a sincere heart (Matthew 15:8-9).

Note that Jesus used *proskuneo* for worship, referring more to inward spiritual attitude than to external acts. He focused on individual devotion rather than external location.

Perhaps the best understanding of worship "in spirit and truth" would be to understand that "in spirit" means in the realm of the spirit. Each of us has a spirit. It is our identity, that which wills, our volition. Paul wrote, "For who among men knows the thoughts of a man except the spirit of the man, which is in him?" (1 Corinthians 2:11).

God is identified as a spiritual being. Relating to Him in worship involves our spirit. Worshiping God means we are on the same spiritual wavelength. In worship the spirit of a person comes into fellowship with God the Spirit.

Worshiping "in truth" involves the right acts and the right forms, but the focus of the passage probably goes further, involving the truthfulness, sincerity and genuineness of the inner person in worship – the spiritual integrity of an honest heart.

Jesus exposed the worship error of insincerity so common among the Pharisees and scribes: "This people honors Me with their lips, but their heart is far away from Me. But in vain do they worship Me, teaching as doctrines the precepts of men" (Matthew 15:8-9).

They were insincere. They used the right words but did not mean them. What they were doing was not truthful worship, it was "word-only" worship. No matter how beautiful the words, no matter how expensive the offering, no matter how elaborate the surroundings, God does not accept worship unless it comes from the sincere inner spirit of a person. David expressed this in his penitent Psalm:

> For Thou dost not delight in sacrifice, otherwise I
>   would give it;
> Thou art not pleased with burnt offering.
> The sacrifices of God are a broken spirit;
> A broken and a contrite heart, O God, Thou wilt
>   not despise.
>
> (Psalm 51:16-17)

Worship is the genuine willful expression of our spirit in ways God has revealed in His Word.

CORINTHIAN WORSHIP PROBLEMS

Worship perversions usually come from one of two directions: experiential or rationalistic. The experiential is usually identified with the subjective and the emotional; it can become a problem with what sociologists call "right brain" people. The rationalistic is usually identified with objective forms and rational thinking; it can become a problem with what sociologists call "left brain" people. True worship, however, is neither "right brain" or "left brain." It is "total brain."

Both the subjective and objective, both the experiential and the rational are involved in worship. Irrational experiential excitement is not worship. Neither are cold, meaningless rituals worship. The church at Corinth had problems with both of these worship abuses.

The abuse of spiritual gifts seemed to appeal to "right brain" Christians who exalted the subjective and emotional. The Corinthian Christians seemed to be reverting to their experiential pagan background. Paul suggested this in the first part of his corrective teachings: "You know that when you were pagans, you were led astray to the dumb idols, however you were led" (1 Corinthians 12:2). The Greek mystery religions focused on the experiential. The Dionysian devotees would get drunk and believed the spirits of the wine they drank would be *en theos* – "god-in-ness." The devotees of Eleusian rites would be whipped up into an emotional frenzy through their pagan ceremonies. The practices of some voodoo and spiritualists ceremonies imitate these ancient pagan rites. Their purpose was to experience an emotional release and then interpret it as union with God.

The abuse of the miraculous spiritual gift of speaking in foreign languages provided a temptation to imitate experiential pagan worship. Paul corrected them. Worship needed to be rational – prayers and singing were to be done with the spirit and understanding (1 Corinthians 14:15-16). Worship needed to build up others – all things were to be done for edification (1 Corinthians 14:26). Worship was to be orderly – all things were to be done in a proper and orderly manner (1 Corinthians 14:40).

Worship must not be robbed of its emotional content or made void of feelings. Recognize, however, that worship is expression, not impression. It is the rational expression of the spirit of man before the holiness of God. It is God-centered, not human-centered.

The same congregation in which some were reverting to pagan ecstasy had others who were practicing the forms of worship while forgetting the content. They had forgotten the meaning of the Lord's Supper:

> When you come together as a church, I hear that divisions exist among you; and in part, I believe it. …
> Therefore when you meet together, it is not to eat the Lord's Supper, for in your eating each one takes his own supper first; and one is hungry and another is drunk (1 Corinthians 11:18, 20-21).

We cannot know all that was involved in the division that resulted in the Corinthians' observing the Lord's Supper at separate times, but Paul said it was wrong. It was not because of crowded conditions in the place of assembly or a work schedule that made it necessary for them to assemble at different hours. It was because of divisiveness that some refused to wait for others. Refusing to commune with fellow Christians because of a divisive spirit was wrong then and still is.

Some people have suggested, with merit, that Paul was referring not only to the body of Christ on the cross and in the bread, but also to the body of Christ, the church. The context of division and different factions partaking of the Lord's Supper at different times supports this view. Paul admonished them clearly: "For he who eats and drinks, eats and drinks judgment to himself, if he does not judge the body rightly. ... So then, my brethren, when you come together to eat, wait for one another" (1 Corinthians 11:29, 33). They needed not only the right form of the Lord's Supper but also the right spiritual content. They needed to commune not only with the body of Christ crucified on the cross but also with the body of Christ that met together as the church.

Worship embraces both attitude and form. The most common words translated "worship" reflect this. Worship is in spirit and in truth. Arising from the inner spirit of man, worship is genuine in its expression. Worship is both experiential and rational. It is sinful to divide Christians into psychological factions of "right brain" and "left brain" individuals or into cultural divisions of traditional and contemporary worshipers.

QUESTIONS

1. What do the two main words translated "worship" inform us on the nature of worship?
2. Review the four teachings about worship in John 4:18-24 and discuss their relevance today.
3. Are there contemporary "worship" practices similar to the abuse of spiritual gifts at Corinth?
4. Are there contemporary "worship" practices similar to the perversion of the Lord's Supper at Corinth?
5. Identify some of the lessons about worship, individually and as a church, that need to be learned today.
6. Name some ways of helping to keep balance between the external forms and the internal attitudes of worship.

CHAPTER THREE

WHAT WORSHIP INVOLVES

Psalm 51:3-12; Isaiah 6:1-5; Matthew 4:8-10;
Colossians 2:20-23; Hebrews 5:7-8; 12:18-29

Sometimes the study of worship is no more than the pooling of ignorance in an "I think" tank or experiential testimonies of religious feelings. If the study of worship revolves around expressing such personal, subjective feelings, the results will be conflicting and confusing.

Many devotional exercises that are called "Worship of God" are not. A performance of Handel's "Messiah" might stir the emotions but falls short of worship. Listeners are "impressed" rather than "expressing" praise. Also, repeating memorized devotional words of a gospel song without meaning them falls short of worship. The heart, spirit and mind are not involved. The right object, the right attitudes and the right forms must come together to make worship acceptable to God. Examples of unacceptable worship abound in Scriptures.

WORSHIP PERVERSIONS

The first recorded act of worship perversion was by Adam's oldest son, Cain. He offered a sacrifice of the fruit of the ground. His brother, Abel, offered a sacrifice of the firstlings of his flock. The Lord "had regard for Abel and for his offering; but for Cain and for his offering He had no regard" (Genesis 4:4). We do not know why God accepted Abel's offering and rejected Cain's offering. We do know, however, that Abel's offering was "by faith," implying that Cain's offering was not "by faith" (Hebrews 11:4). Abel's offering resulted from hearing and doing the will of God. The Scriptures teach that faith comes by hearing the word of God (Romans 10:17) and is perfected by doing the will of God (James 2:22). Cain's offering was not "by faith." This example shows that it does make a difference how one worships.

Nadab and Abihu, the sons of Aaron, offered strange fire "which God commanded not" while burning incense in the tabernacle worship (Leviticus 10:1-2). They failed to respect the prohibitive silence of God's commands and introduced fire God had not authorized. God struck them dead with fire from heaven because of this presumptuous sin.

Another incident during the wilderness wanderings demonstrated how something God gave as good can become bad because of worship perversion. The children of Israel murmured in the wilderness after leaving Mount Hor. God sent fiery serpents into the camp to punish them. Many died. The people asked Moses to plead with God that the serpents might be removed. God told Moses, "Make a fiery serpent, and set it on a standard; and it shall come about, that everyone who is bitten, when he looks at it, he shall live" (Numbers 21:8). Moses did what God said, and the people were saved.

For a while there was no mention of what was done with this bronze serpent. Much later, however, it turned up again during the reign of king Hezekiah. Regarding his reform to purge the land from idols, the Scriptures say, "He also broke in pieces the bronze serpent that Moses had made, for until those days the sons of Israel burned incense to it" (2 Kings 18:4). Israel made an idol out of something God had given as an expression of His mercy. People do similar things today.

King Saul presumptuously offered sacrifices without divine authority. He was not a priest, yet he took it upon himself to fulfill a priestly function in what he perceived as an emergency. Samuel, the prophet-priest, had not arrived to offer a sacrifice before Israel went to war with the Philistines. The army was deserting. Saul took matters into his own hands and made a sacrifice. He tried to excuse his conduct to Samuel by saying, "I forced myself and offered the burnt offering" (1 Samuel 13:12). Despite his alleged good intentions, Samuel told him, "You have not kept the commandment of the Lord your God, … now your kingdom shall not endure" (vv. 13-14). Later, Saul again neglected to do "all" that God told him to do in destroying the Amalekites; Samuel reminded Saul, "Behold, to obey is better than sacrifice, And to heed than the fat of rams. For rebellion is as the sin of divination, and insubordination is as iniquity and idolatry" (15:22-23)

God expects worship to be done as He has commanded. No matter how sincere the motive, no matter what might be the trends of the culture, no matter what the people desire, God wants worship to be done His way.

Worship perversion involves not only external forms but also the internal attitudes of the worshiper. Isaiah spoke of sin as the cause of estrangement from God: "But your iniquities have made a separation between you and your God, and your sins have hidden His face from you, so that He does not hear" (Isaiah 59:2). Impenitent sinfulness and worship are mutually exclusive. We cannot be a true worshiper of God and a servant of the devil at the same time.

Worship is also flawed by the neglect of justice and mercy to God's children. We cannot love God and hate our brother (1 John 4:20). Amos prophesied against those who sought to worship God but neglected justice and righteousness:

> Even though you offer up to Me burnt offerings and your grain offerings, I will not accept them; And I will not even look at the peace offerings of your fatlings.

Take away from Me the noise of your songs; I will not even listen to the sound of your harps. But let justice roll down like waters and righteousness like an ever-flowing stream (Amos 5:22-24).

THE OBJECT OF WORSHIP

Heinrich Greeven, in his article on *proskuneo* in *Kittel's Theological Dictionary*, makes this observation: "When the NT uses *proskuneo*, the object is always something – truly or supposedly – divine" (*TDNT*, Vol. VI, p. 763).

Peter refused worship (*proskuneo*) from Cornelius (Acts 10:25). An angel refused worship (*proskuneo*) from the apostle John. The angel told John, "Do not do that; I am a fellow servant of yours and your brethren who hold the testimony of Jesus; worship God" (Revelation 19:10).

When tempted to worship the devil in exchange for rulership of all the kingdoms of the world, Jesus quoted Moses and said, "For it is written, 'You shall worship the Lord your God, and serve Him only'" (Matthew 4:10). Jesus understood the silence of the Scriptures to be exclusive and prohibitive. Moses did not have to name all of the gods of the Moabites, the Hittites and the Amalekites. He affirmed who was to be worshiped and that excluded all others.

The one and only object of worship is God. We stand before Him in awe because of His power, His majesty, His glory and His grace. He alone is worthy to be the object of our devotion and praise.

AWESOME WORSHIP

Worship is not a dialogue between equals. God is God, and we are human. God is pure spirit; we are flesh and blood. God is Creator, and we are creatures. God knows all, and we are ignorant of all things except what God has revealed in nature and in His Word. God is good, and we are sinful. God is without beginning or end; we are bound by time and matter.

As humans, we prostrate ourselves before Him in humility because of His power and majesty. As humans, we are full of wonder and awe because of His glory and grace. As humans, we submit to His will because of His steadfast love. Worship is the natural response when we, as His creatures, come into His presence. It is motivated by the awesomeness experienced when humanity engages divinity. This awesomeness can be described as dread, fear, respect and reverence.

The awesomeness of God is reflected in the calling of Moses. He stood on holy ground in the presence of God. He took off his shoes and hid his face. Awe, humility and submission overwhelmed his spirit:

> And the angel of the Lord appeared to him in a blazing fire from the midst of a bush; and he looked, and behold, the bush was burning with fire, yet the bush was not consumed. So Moses said, "I must turn aside now, and see this marvelous sight, why the bush is not burned up." When the Lord saw that he turned aside to look, God called to him from the midst of the bush, and said, "Moses, Moses!" And he said, "Here I am." Then He said, "Do not come near here; remove your sandals from your feet, for the place on which you are standing is holy ground." He said also, "I am the God of your father, the God of Abraham, the God of Isaac, and the God of Jacob." Then Moses hid his face, for he was afraid to look at God (Exodus 3:2-6).

Moses stood in fear before the presence of God, not because of the miracle of the burning bush, but more than that – he recognized that he was standing in the presence of the immortal, eternal, spiritual God.

The awesomeness of God is reflected in the giving of the law on Sinai. God came down to man and gave a holy law to make a holy nation. The Israelites experienced an awesome wonder:

> For you have not come to a mountain that may be touched and to a blazing fire, and to darkness and gloom and whirlwind, and to the blast of a trumpet and the sound of words which sound was such that those who heard begged that no further word be spoken to them. For they could not bear the command, "If even

a beast touches the mountain, it will be stoned." And
so terrible was the sight, that Moses said, "I am full of
fear and trembling." ... For our God is a consuming
fire (Hebrews 12:18-21, 29).

Words of holy terror describe this awesome, fearful, majestic
event of God giving the law at Sinai. Even Moses trembled.

The awesomeness of God is reflected, too, in the call of Isaiah.
God manifested Himself in the temple, and Isaiah saw His majestic glory. He described the event in picturesque language:

I saw the Lord sitting on a throne, lofty and exalted,
with the train of His robe filling the temple. Seraphim
stood above Him, each having six wings: with two he
covered his face, and with two he covered his feet, and
with two he flew. And one called out to another and
said, "Holy, Holy, Holy, is the Lord of hosts, The whole
earth is full of His glory." And the foundations of the
thresholds trembled at the voice of him who called out,
while the temple was filling with smoke. Then I said,
"Woe is me, for I am ruined! Because I am a man of
unclean lips, And I live among a people of unclean lips;
For my eyes have seen the King, the Lord of hosts"
(Isaiah 6:1-5).

Isaiah experienced God's power, glory, majesty, holiness as well
as what might be described as holy terror because of God's awesome presence. The Lord sat on a lofty throne, His robe was so
magnificent that its train filled the temple. He was surrounded
with glorious spiritual beings, one of which sang praises of His
holiness, power and glory. His voice vibrated so much that the
thresholds trembled, and smoke filled the temple. The awesomeness of this vision humbled Isaiah so much that he confessed
his unworthiness because he had seen the King, the Lord of hosts.

The above scenes reflect the humble, awesome submission of
persons in the presence of God. This same response should appear when we come into His presence in worship.

God is above and beyond all things. He is before the beginning and after the end. By His power He spoke the worlds into

existence, and yet by His grace He reaches us. Like David, we wonder:

> When I consider Thy heavens, the work of Thy
>   fingers,
> The moon and the stars, which Thou hast or-
>   dained;
> What is man, that Thou dost take thought of him?
> And the son of man, that Thou dost care for him?
>   (Psalm 8:3-4)

No words can express His majesty. No phrase can describe His holiness. In our attempts to give Him praise, we always encounter a limitation of language. Even if we could use correct words, we could not understand the depth of their meaning. We stand in awe, but we take comfort in the promise of the Scripture:

> [W]e do not know how to pray as we should, but the Spirit Himself intercedes for us with groanings too deep for words; and He who searches the hearts knows what the mind of the Spirit is, because He intercedes for the saints according to the will of God (Romans 8:26-27).

HUMBLE SUBMISSION

Growing out of a heart filled with awe is a spirit of willing and humble submission – essential elements in true worship. Notice this spirit of humble submission in Samuel's response when the Lord called him as a mere child. He said, "Speak, Lord, for Thy servant is listening" (1 Samuel 3:9). This was the spirit of Isaiah's response to the Lord's questions, "Whom shall I send, and who will go for Us?" Isaiah replied, "Here am I. Send me!" (Isaiah 6:8).

Humble submission in worship exists in its highest form in the ministry of Jesus. Three times He prayed in the garden, "My Father, if it is possible, let this cup pass from Me; yet not as I will, but as Thou will" (Matthew 26:39ff). The yearnings of His humanity were expressed in His prayers, but His inner spirit yielded to the will of God, whatever that will might be. He prayed, "Thy will be done." After His struggle of praying in the garden,

He could then awaken His disciples and say, "Arise, let us be going; behold, the one who betrays Me is at hand!" (26:46).

The writer of Hebrews used Jesus' prayer in Gethsemane to show the importance of combining deep spiritual piety with humble, submissive obedience:

> In the days of His flesh, He offered up both prayers and supplications with loud crying and tears to the One able to save Him from death, and He was heard because of His piety. Although He was a Son, He learned obedience from the things which He suffered (Hebrews 5:7-8).

Jesus' greatest act of worship was the offering of Himself as a sin offering for the sins of the world. Despite His tearful prayers in the garden, despite the shame of the cross, despite the suffering He was to endure in both His body and His spirit, Jesus went to the cross in obedience to the will of God. In contrast to the inadequate blood of unwilling bulls and goats, Christ "through the eternal Spirit offered Himself without blemish to God" (Hebrews 9:14). Paul described this act of humble submission: "He humbled Himself by becoming obedient to the point of death, even death on a cross" (Philippians 2:8). Jesus' teaching and example both show that our relationship to God in worship does not merely rest upon the awe we experience in His presence; it also rests upon our humble submission to His will.

Daniel saw a vision in which God revealed to him what would happen to his people in the latter days. The vision was so awesome that Daniel shook with terror and fell on his face to the ground. The messenger told him to stand up and then said to him, "Do not be afraid, Daniel, for from the first day that you set your heart on understanding this and on humbling yourself before your God, your words were heard, and I have come in response to your words" (Daniel 10:12). Worship involves a willing and humble submission to the will of God. Worship is not doing worship things the way you like it or even the way most people like it. It means doing God-ordained worship in God's way. No substitutes are allowed. No changes will be tolerated. It involves a willing humble submission to His will.

The false teachers reflected in Colossians apparently had willful worship problems. They were teaching asceticism. It did not come from the Lord, but from the commandments and teachings of men. It was supposed to be religious and had the appearance of wisdom, but Paul called it "self-made religion": "These are matters which have, to be sure, the appearance of wisdom in self-made religion and self-abasement and severe treatment of the body, but are of no value against fleshly indulgence" (Colossians 2:23).

The King James Version translated *ethelothperkia* as "will worship." The New American Standard Bible translated it as "self-made religion." Both are good translations since the word is a compound from *ethelo* meaning "will" and *threskeia* meaning "religious worship." Some of the Christians at Colossae were doing what they wanted to do in worship. It was "worship like you like it," without regard for the will of the Lord.

How similar their teaching was to some contemporary worship trends. Those who advocate such trends seek to justify on the basis of "I want it, I like it, I'm going to do it." This attitude is "will worship." It is the very opposite to humble, willing submission. Paul corrected the pre-Gnostics at Colossae by writing this admonition: "See to it that no one takes you captive through philosophy and empty deception, according to the tradition of men, according to the elementary principles of the world, rather than according to Christ" (Colossians 2:8). The same teaching is relevant today and exposes willful, self-centered, secularized worship as being rebellion against the high and holy God.

Contrition and Celebration

Worship expresses the spirit of a man. It can involve the joys of victory and the anguish of defeat. Sometimes tears fill our eyes as sorrow flows from the spirit. Sometimes worship overflows from a grateful heart with thanksgiving. Sometimes we plead for God's blessings to relieve our pain. There are no times when worship cannot fill the needs of the soul.

David prayed with a heart of contrition and words of submission as in humility he sought the forgiveness of God:

> For I know my transgressions,
> And my sin is ever before me.
> Against Thee, Thee only, I have sinned,
> And done what is evil in Thy sight. ...
> Create in me a clean heart, O God,
> And renew a steadfast spirit within me.
> Do not cast me away from Thy presence
> And do not take Thy Holy Spirit from me.
> Restore to me the joy of Thy salvation
> And sustain me with a willing spirit.
>   (Psalm 51:3-4, 10-12)

Israel sang songs of joyful celebration as they journeyed to Jerusalem for their feast days. Psalm 100 must have been one of those songs.

> Shout joyfully to the Lord, all the earth.
> Serve the Lord with gladness;
> Come before Him with joyful singing.
> Know that the Lord Himself is God;
> It is He who has made us, and not we ourselves;
> We are His people and the sheep of His pasture.
>   (Psalm 100:1-3)

Worship fits every mood and is appropriate on every occasion. James showed that worship is the expression of the soul in the extremes of both suffering and cheerfulness: "Is anyone among you suffering? Let him pray. Is anyone cheerful? Let him sing praises" (James 5:13). In worship we have communion with God who cares for us and controls the universe.

SUMMARY

Perverted worship is as old as Cain. God did not regard his offering. Every conceivable kind of perverted worship has been practiced by people who refuse to give awesome, humble submission in worship. It begins with neglect, it moves on to human speculation, it results in idolatry and it finally ends by God's giving them up to their own reprobate minds.

Two primary attitudes are involved in true worship. First, there is a sense of awe in coming into the presence of the high and holy God. Second, there is an attitude of willful, humble submission to God – a willingness to worship the only true God in the only way He wishes to be worshiped.

QUESTIONS

1. Identify the worship error in the following events:
   - The sacrifice of Cain
   - The incense offering of Nadab and Abihu
   - The brazen serpent put up by Moses
   - The sacrifice made by King Saul
2. What lesson can we learn about the prohibitive silence of Scriptures in Jesus' response to the devil's temptation?
3. Discuss the attitude Christians should have in worship.
4. Show ways people strive to stimulate awe in worshiping God.
5. Show ways people negate awe in worshiping God.
6. Discuss the prayer Jesus offered in the Garden of Gethsemane (Matthew 26:36ff). When and how was it answered?

CHAPTER FOUR

WORSHIP: ACTS OR LIFESTYLE?

*John 16:2; Acts 8:27; 24:10; Romans 12:1-2; Galatians 2:20;
Philippians 2:17; 1 Peter 2:5; Hebrews 13:15-16*

Sometimes a fog of confusion obscures both the nature of worship and its practice. This confusion centers on both its meaning and its purpose. Does worship mean living a consecrated, holy life, or does it mean to commune with God in ways He has decreed and in a mindset of awesome, humble submission? Does it mean both?

IS ALL OF LIFE WORSHIP?

We commonly hear, "Don't you know that all of life is worship?" in discussions of worship forms. My response is: "No, it isn't; and yes, it is." It depends on what we mean and understand by the term "worship."

All of life is not worship if it is understood to be like a holy, consecrated animal offered on the brazen altar by priests in the temple. Worship by the patriarchs or by priests was specific acts, done in specific ways, at a specific time, at a specific place and by spe-

cific people. It was holy acts. The patriarchs or priests would have
sinned had they deviated from the way God commanded them.
Moses taught very specifically about how to worship:

> You shall utterly destroy all the places where the na-
> tions whom you shall dispossess serve their gods, ...
> And you shall tear down their altars and smash their
> sacred pillars and burn their Asherim with fire, and
> you shall cut down the engraved images of their gods,
> ... You shall not do at all what we are doing here to-
> day, every man doing whatever is right in his own eyes;
> ... Be careful that you do not offer your burnt offer-
> ings in every cultic place you see, but in the place which
> the Lord chooses ... beware ... that you do not inquire
> after their gods, saying, "How do these nations serve
> their gods, that I also may do likewise?" ... Whatever
> I command you, you shall be careful to do; you shall
> not add to nor take away from it (Deuteronomy 12:2-
> 3, 8, 13, 30, 32).

God told the Israelites where, what, how and when to worship.
This was a command of God. It was not "whatever is right in
[their] own eyes." It was not the way the "nations serve their
gods." Israel was neither to add to nor to take away from what
God commanded.

At the same time, all acts, thoughts and words of a Christian
should be holy and consecrated to God like a sacrifice. The
Scriptures use worship words and sacrificial language to describe
this pious conduct, but we should not confuse it with deeper and
more specific acts of worship such as praying, singing and observing the Lord's Supper. These specific acts of worship must
involve a willing spirit, an understanding mind and a feeling heart.

My understanding of lifestyle worship is "informal acts of pious living." The willful spirit, the conscious mind and the feeling
heart need not be involved in such worship.

One might understand lifestyle worship as an analogy to the
external acts of worship in the temple. It would be wrong, however, to equate it with rational, conscious worship done in awesome, humble submission to God. We should not confuse willful

acts of devotion with a holy lifestyle stemming from a faith commitment in the past. Both may be called "worship" – the acts because they result in immediate communion with God through Jesus and the Holy Spirit, and the lifestyle because, in a metaphorical sense, it represents the totality of a holy life sacrificed to God.

LIFESTYLE WORSHIP

Paul's admonition to the church at Rome is a key passage in discussing lifestyle worship:

> I urge you therefore, brethren, by the mercies of God, to present your bodies a living and holy sacrifice, acceptable to God, which is your spiritual service of worship. And do not be conformed to this world, but be transformed by the renewing of your mind, that you may prove what the will of God is, that which is good and acceptable and perfect (Romans 12:1-2).

Note three things from this passage.

First, Paul contrasts the worshiper's living body with a dead animal sacrifice. The animal is dead; the Christian's body is alive. The animal is a physical thing; the worshiper is a holy being, "set apart for a sacred use."

Second, if the animal sacrifice should be good, acceptable and perfect, the same applies to the conduct of the worshiper. We are not to "conform to the world," but be "transformed by the renewing of [our] mind." Notice the inside/outside change in lifestyle. It is a change from the profane to the holy, from death to living, from conforming to renewing.

Third, the phrase "spiritual service of worship" is a translation of *latreian*. As already noted, *latreuein* means "to serve or worship cultically, especially by sacrifice." As the priests in the temple performed cultic acts of worship daily in the temple, the worshiper should daily offer life as a sacrifice to God.

Paul also used an analogy of "crucifixion" in speaking of his surrender to the will of God: "I have been crucified with Christ; and it is no longer I who live, but Christ lives in me; and the life which I now live in the flesh I live by faith in the Son of God, who loved me, and delivered Himself up for me" (Galatians 2:20). Paul was not speaking of a literal, physical crucifixion. He was only using the physical reality of a crucifixion as an analogy to show his total commitment to the Lord. In the same way, we can use the physical, spiritual reality of worship as an analogy to show that our life is under the Lordship of Jesus.

Stan Mitchell recently observed the subtle meaning of the two primary words that are translated "worship" in the New Testament:

> The two major words are *proskuneo*, which describes the ancient practice of "prostrating oneself before a person and kissing his feet ... and *latreuo*, a word that refers to service offered in honor of God." The verb, *proskuneo* ... describes worship in what we might call its purest sense, the moment when a supplicant throws his heart and soul before God Almighty in an act of honor that is absolute. The second word translated "worship," *latreuo*, is a verb that indicates the "carrying out of religious duties." The former seems to refer more strictly to what we might call a "formal" worship time, while the latter extends to the way we live and serve the Lord (from an unpublished research paper).

No one should take this worship-sacrifice analogy literally. Paul is not telling his readers to lay their bodies on an altar to be consumed by fire. He is using the sacrifice motif to show that a Christian should live a holy, consecrated life. A committed life of humble submission and service is the sacrificial offering.

This word *latreuo* is used along with the same sacrifice motif in other passages to describe "acts showing commitment to God." Jesus told His disciples on one occasion about their coming persecution: "They will make you outcasts from the synagogue, but an hour is coming for everyone who kills you to think that he is offering service to God" (John 16:2). The word translated "offering service" in this text is *latreian*. The perverted minds of those who opposed Christ thought that the murder of His followers would be an act of piety.

Both Paul and Peter used the sacrifice analogy for pious acts of commitment: "But even if I am being poured out as a drink offering upon the sacrifice and service of your faith, I rejoice" (Philippians 2:17) and "you also, as living stones, are being built up as a spiritual house for a holy priesthood, to offer up spiritual sacrifices acceptable to God through Jesus Christ" (1 Peter 2:5).

Paul was not speaking literally of his being poured out as a drink offering. He was describing the total commitment and holy consecration he had in his relationship with the church at Philippi.

Peter emphasized that Christian sacrifices are spiritual. Like the animals sacrificed at the temple, the spiritual sacrifices of a Christian are healthy and holy.

The book of Hebrews brings together worship that involves both specific acts of praise and general pious service. Both are called sacrifices: "Through Him then, let us continually offer up a sacrifice of praise to God, that is, the fruit of lips that give thanks to His name. And do not neglect doing good and sharing; for with such sacrifices God is pleased" (Hebrews 13:15-16).

Christian sacrifices do not involve cows and goats offered on an altar in a temple. The sacrifices that a Christian offers include both the acts of worship involving spirit-willed praise and devotion as well as doing good and sharing in the name of the Lord. One is a sacrifice of praise, and the other is a sacrifice of service. We should not confuse the figurative and general way of presenting our bodies as living, holy sacrifices in a spiritual service of worship with the more specific spirit-willed, mind-understood and heart-felt literal sense of worship.

Several Bible characters drew near to God in this special sense. Consider the story of Abraham and Isaac on Mount Moriah: "And Abraham said to his young men, 'Stay here with the donkey, and I and the lad will go yonder; and we will worship and return to you'" (Genesis 22:5). Abraham was not worshiping when he spoke to the young men. He was worshiping when he performed God's prescribed acts.

David went "to worship" (2 Samuel 12:20). The Ethiopian eunuch came to Jerusalem "to worship" (Acts 8:27ff). Paul told Felix that he went up to Jerusalem "to worship" (Acts 24:10ff). More is involved in this kind of worship than everyday piety.

There is a general way in which we offer *latreuo* to God in acts of daily piety. The Scriptures employ worship words and sacrificial language to describe this. There is also a specific way in which we offer *proskuneo* to God with a willing spirit, a rational mind and an aware consciousness. We worship God in awesome, humble submission.

We cannot substitute acts of pious service for spiritual "fruit of the lips" sacrifice. Neither can we substitute words of worshipful praise for pious acts of sharing service. Like faith and works, they are both necessary, but different. One is literal; the other is analogous. One focuses on external acts of pious living; the other focuses on inner, awesome devotion and praise before the high and holy God. Failing to distinguish between a life of piety and acts of worship presents serious logical problems.

We need to note the consequences of the foolish concept that all of life is worship. This reasoning opens the door for anything that a person wants to do, if it is called "worship." Even murder could be "offering service to God" (John 16:2). If all of life is worship, then we could worship any way we wanted without restraint.

An old but true saying comes to mind: "That which means everything, means nothing." If we define a word so broadly as to mean everything, it ceases to mean anything. If all of life is worship, then it makes no difference how we worship. We could worship by bowing down before an idol; we could worship by giving ecstatic utterances and calling it the voice of God; we could worship by drinking wine and believe that the effects of the wine are the divine presence; we could worship by burning incense or playing on an instrument to create an experience of awe; we could worship by dancing to stimulate an emotional frenzy.

On and on we could go and consider anything and everything as worshiping God. But if we define worship as meaning everything, it ends up meaning nothing at all.

Do we fail to regard the will of the Lord in this matter? Some of the final words Joshua spoke to Israel affirm the need of being faithful in the exercise of worship: "Now, therefore, fear the Lord and serve Him in sincerity and truth" (Joshua 24:14).

Worship does not casually and unconsciously happen without our exercising our willing spirit, rational mind and feeling heart. In general, all of life should be lived in an awesome, humble submissive response to God's grace and goodness. This response should involve ethics, morality, benevolence, compassion and brotherly love. All of these, and more, should exist in a spiritual commitment to live a holy consecrated life. Peter affirmed that holiness is the lifestyle of all of God's children:

> As obedient children, do not be conformed to the former lusts which were yours in ignorance, but like the Holy One who called you, be holy yourselves also in all your behavior; because it is written, "You shall be holy, for I am holy" (1 Peter 1:14-16).

Worship words and sacrificial language may be used to describe this piety as worship in a symbolic sense. But it would be difficult to see how daily pious conduct mixed with unwilling, unconscious and unfeeling thoughts and deeds could be called worship in its more fundamental sense. How can we worship God without wanting to or trying to?

ARE THERE ACTS OF WORSHIP?

Most readers have heard sermons identifying five acts of Christian worship. This list of "five acts" is sometimes ridiculed as being legalistic and ritualistic.

The technical accuracy of "acts of worship" in some situations can be questioned. It really depends on how we define "acts" and how we define "worship." If "acts" are no more that mindless, meaningless rituals, then they cannot be classified as worship. If "worship" is defined so broadly that it excludes nothing, then worship has no meaning. If, however, these terms are defined so that the average person will understand the most common meaning, the use of the phrase "acts of worship" is correct. The five acts are:

- Singing to God and sometimes to one another;
- Praying to God and sometimes with one another;

- Communing with God and His children in the Lord's Supper;
- Sharing with God and others in giving;
- Listening to God in reading or hearing His Word.

None of these acts is specifically called "worship" in Scripture. We call them "acts" or "items" of worship because they fit into what worship is and does. They are acts of praise and devotion from the spirit of man directed to the only true and living God. They are God-affirmed means of communion with God on a spiritual level. They are things we are commanded to do. In the faith and works parallel, they are works that are commanded of those claiming faith. Kerry Anderson, president of the Gospel Advocate Company, uses a slightly different model:

- Talking to God in prayer and praise;
- Listening to God in Bible reading and proclamation;
- Communing with God in the Lord's Supper;
- Submitting to God in response to this fellowship of worship; adjusting our sense of relationship by giving and doing.

The phrase "acts of worship" has experienced some bad press by those who either misunderstand or willfully reject its intended meaning. One could just as well call what is being done "activities of devotion," which would mean the same thing. To someone familiar with the psychology of religion, the acts of worship could be called "the awesome response to the numinous" and convey the same idea. The phrase "activities of devotion" might appeal to the pious monk. The phrase "human response to the wholly other" might appeal to the theologian. But to the average person, the phrase "acts of worship" communicates. These activities are specific, God-authorized acts arising from the human spirit to give homage to God. They happen at certain times and places, have a beginning and end, and are done according to the will of God. The fact that some like to use this phrase in disdain and falsely identify it with cold, empty rituals of meaningless words should not keep us from using it.

As already shown, the words translated "worship" convey two ideas – a sense of awe and humble submission and formal acts of cultic service. All five acts of worship involve these attributes.

Singing is an act of worship arising from our spirit's desire to praise God and edify others. The songs give honor and glory to God. His presence is so awesome that, like the angels in heaven, we sing to praise His glory.

Praying is another act of worship arising from our desire to express praise, petitions and penitence to God. The focus is to praise God and to make petitions for ourselves and others. We stand in awe that God – who numbers the hairs on our head and realizes every sparrow that falls – hears and answers our prayers.

The Lord's Supper is a third act of worship arising from our spirit. In it we commune with Christ and His church. It is awesome to realize that we are in the presence of the loving Savior and are remembering His death on the cross. It is a time of holy and hushed communion with our risen Lord who will someday be our Judge.

Giving is a fourth act of worship arising from our spirit. The Christians in Macedonia gave generously because they "first gave themselves to the Lord" (2 Corinthians 8:5). Gratitude, humility and love flow together to find expression in the gifts we give to Him who made and sustains all things as they are.

Fifth, listening to the Word of God is an act of worship. This language is received, not as the words of men, but as it is in truth, the Word of God (1 Thessalonians 2:13). We listen in awe and humble submission, for it is the Lord who speaks.

If the universe came into existence by the word of God, and it did; if God's plan for the ages is contained in His Word, and it is; then what reverence we should have when God speaks in His Word!

While acts of worship are required by God, they do not constitute the totality of the godly acts done by a Christian but are one part of the total God wants.

These acts of worship were integral to the New Testament church. They are specifically identified in Paul's Corinthian correspondence regarding abuse of worship.

The church at Corinth perverted song and prayer. The experience of the gift of tongues had so captivated people's attention that they forgot the purpose of singing and praying. Some did not understand what they were saying, and listeners could not understand the meaning. Paul corrected them in their worship error: "I shall pray with the spirit and I shall pray with the mind also; I shall sing with the spirit and I shall sing with the mind also" (1 Corinthians 14:15).

The church at Corinth perverted the Lord's Supper because of divisiveness in the congregation. We do not know the reasons for the factions, but we do know a result – Christians were not observing the Lord's Supper at the same time. Paul corrected them in their worship error: "So then, my brethren, when you come together to eat, wait for one another" (1 Corinthians 11:33). Their divisiveness conflicted with one of the purposes of the Lord's Supper. The weekly event was supposed to allow them to "commune" with both the Lord and His church. Paul corrected the Corinthians on this point:

> Is not the cup of blessing which we bless a sharing in the blood of Christ? Is not the bread which we break a sharing in the body of Christ? Since there is one bread, we who are many are one body; for we all partake of the one bread (1 Corinthians 10:16-17).

The word translated "sharing" is *koinonia* in the Greek text and is translated "communion" in the New King James Version. The act of worshiping in the Lord's Supper is both communion with Jesus and His church.

The church at Corinth perverted the prophesying of God's word. Some tried to prophesy while other prophets were speaking. Some talked too long and refused to share their speaking time. The result: confusion. Paul corrected them in their worship error:

> Let all things be done for edification. ... And let two or three prophets speak, and let the others pass judgment. But if a revelation is made to another who is seated, let the first keep silent (1 Corinthians 14:26, 29-30).

The Corinthians needed instruction about their giving. Paul, who was taking up a collection for the poor saints in Jerusalem, devoted the equivalent of two chapters (8 and 9) in 2 Corinthians discussing the motive, means and rewards of giving. In his first letter he was concerned that they might not be doing what they needed to have the funds ready when Paul arrived, so he wrote, "On the first day of every week, let each one of you put aside and save, as he may prosper, that no collections be made when I come" (1 Corinthians 16:2).

Greater attention will be given to these avenues of worship later in the book, but the purpose now is to show that they are worship in that they are acts of awesome, humble submission (*proskuneo*) to God.

The question posed at the beginning of this chapter was: Does worship mean living a consecrated, holy life, or does it mean communing with God in ways He has decreed and in a mindset of awesome, humble submission? Or does it mean both?

It means both! They are different aspects of the same thing. One consists of an inward attitude of spirit, mind and heart seeking communion with God by awesome, humble submission. The other consists of external acts of devotion and service done in the way God has prescribed in response to His grace and goodness. They must not be separated. Neglecting one results in historical monasticism. Neglecting the other results in cold ritualism.

QUESTIONS

1. Discuss the differences in the meanings of the two primary words translated "worship" in the New Testament.
2. List what are generally called "acts of worship" and show that more is involved than mere lifestyle piety.
3. List some worship words and sacrificial language used in the New Testament to show total commitment.
4. What is the logical consequence to the teaching that "all of life is worship?"
5. What does it mean to "come to worship?" Does it involve a certain time and distinct place?
6. What constitutes an act of worship? What are its qualities?

CHAPTER FIVE

WORSHIP AND CULTURE

Matthew 15:1-9; Luke 5:30-39;
2 Thessalonians 2:15; 3:6

Culture influences both the language and forms of worship. We realize this when we participate in the worship assemblies of the church in different geographical areas and with different ethnic and social backgrounds.

In some predominantly African-American assemblies, you notice more exuberance in singing as well as frequent expressions of "Amen" and "Preach on, brother!" punctuating the sermon. Conduct in the assembly will be less formal, and time restraints will be less marked.

In some predominantly mid-American, Anglo, rural or blue-collar assemblies, you will hear Stamps-Baxter songs and more evangelistic preaching. Conduct in the assembly will be open, unsophisticated and practical.

In some assemblies of predominantly college-educated, white-collar professionals in the suburbs, you will notice the prominence of either the old traditional hymns of the 19th century or contemporary praise songs. This will depend on the generational make-up of the church. Preaching will center on contemporary social and theological issues and service. The assembly will be formal and tightly structured.

In some assemblies of the predominantly socially rejected, ethnically diverse and economically poor dwellers of the inner-city, you will hear many songs emphasizing salvation, redemption and heaven. Preaching will probably be emotional and urgent, emphasizing grace and repentance. Conduct in the assembly will lack formality. Those attending will be less formally dressed but will exhibit a spirit of joy, humility and praise.

The above patterns are not necessarily the rule but tend to be frequent scenarios. The more you meet with Christians on foreign soils, the more you notice culture's effects on worship assemblies. Language, ethnic background, political orientation, social structures and former religious traditions all affect their attitudes, language and structure of worship.

An ethnic Jewish congregation in Jerusalem will differ from an ethnic Zulu congregation in the tribal trust land of Zimbabwe, Africa. An ethnic Greek congregation in Athens will differ from an ethnic Indian congregation on a reservation in Arizona.

Cultural differences existed during the apostolic age, too. Some people ate meat, and others did not. Some practiced circumcision, and others did not. Paul, who so effectively taught against transferring the religious practices of Judaism into Christian worship, participated in religious purification in the temple. The Jewish synagogue became a prominent place for early Christians to preach the message of Jesus. How can we make sense of all this? Jesus gave instructions on how to deal with cultural traditions in His teaching on fasting.

TRADITIONS: BOUND OR LOOSED

Jesus taught how to regard religious traditions by His response to a question concerning fasting. His answer was illustrated by the parables of the wineskins and the patched garment. The scribes of the Pharisees, grumbling about Jesus' association with tax collectors and sinners, asked Him a question about fasting:

> And they said to Him, "The disciples of John often fast
> and offer prayers; the disciples of the Pharisees also
> do the same; but Yours eat and drink." And Jesus said
> to them, "You cannot make the attendants of the bride-
> groom fast while the bridegroom is with them, can
> you? But the days will come; and when the bridegroom
> is taken away from them, then they will fast in those
> days" (Luke 5:33-35).

From this narrative we can learn three guidelines about observing human religious traditions in worship.

First, the disciples of Jesus were not to observe any religious
practices because "everybody else is doing it." It makes no difference what other religious people are doing. If there was no authority
for it and no valid religious purpose, it was not to be practiced.

The Israelites used this excuse when pleading for a king. They
asked Samuel to "appoint a king for us to judge us like all the nations" (1 Samuel 8:5). The people of Israel would later confess to
Samuel, "[W]e have added to all our sins this evil by asking for
ourselves a king" (12:19).

Moses had warned Israel about religious compromise with the
Canaanite nations. When they conquered the land, Israel was not
to become involved with their religious culture. Israel was to "ut-
terly destroy them ... make no covenant with them ... not intermarry with them" (Deuteronomy 7:2-3). These acts of compromise would lead to apostasy. Moses warned: "For they will turn
your sons away from following Me to serve other gods" (v. 4).

Israel did not heed this warning. Its history is filled with stories of how it would first associate with idol worshipers, then tolerate their idol worship, and finally begin to practice idolatry.

Second, disciples of Jesus were not to practice fasting merely
because it was the traditional thing to do. The disciples of the
Pharisees fasted. It was an old cultural tradition handed down by
the rabbis from the religious culture of the ancient past. The disciples of John fasted. It was a new tradition handed over from the
contemporary religious culture of the times.

The word translated "tradition" is *paradosis*. It means to "hand
down" or to "hand over" and can refer to that which is either good

or bad. If an act is a human religious tradition, it must not be bound. Jesus expressed this to the Pharisee who criticized His disciples for eating bread with unwashed hands: "[Y]ou invalidate the word of God for the sake of your tradition. ... But in vain do they worship Me, teaching as doctrines the precepts of men" (Matthew 15:6, 9).

If an act is the religious tradition of the apostles, it cannot be loosed. Paul used the formula of "received" and "delivered" to express that which was handed down by Jesus or by His authority:

> For I delivered to you as of first importance what I also received, that Christ died for our sins according to the Scriptures, and that He was buried, and that He was raised on the third day according to the Scriptures (1 Corinthians 15:3-4; see also 11:23).

Human traditions are not to be regarded as religious authority, but traditions coming from the apostles are binding. When we reject them, we reject the authority of Jesus. Paul clearly stated:

> So then, brethren, stand firm and hold to the traditions which you were taught, whether by word of mouth or by letter from us. ... Now we command you, brethren, in the name of our Lord Jesus Christ, that you keep aloof from every brother who leads an unruly life and not according to the tradition which you received from us (2 Thessalonians 2:15; 3:6).

Change in worship practices can be good, bad or neutral. If the change veers from human traditions to the apostolic tradition, it is good. That is called "repentance." If change veers from what Jesus authorized to human cultural traditions, it is bad. That is called "apostasy." If change is only in what expedites a command, it is neutral.

Third, a religious practice must have a valid purpose. Fasting, for example, is an expression of deep religious feelings of sorrow or loss. The disciples of Jesus had no reason to fast while He was with them. They had no sorrow or loss. When He would be taken from them, then they would have a reason to fast.

A valid question to ask when considering any change in worship is, "Why?" That question raises other questions. "Is it more Scriptural?" "Is it more edifying?" "Will it offend another Christian's conscience?" "Is the motive to please God or to please people?"

THE PARABLE OF THE WINESKINS

We must not lift the parable of the wineskins out of its context. It was spoken in response to the question asked by the scribes of the Pharisees, "Why do not your disciples fast like other religious people?" We need to understand and interpret it in this context.

> No one tears a piece from a new garment and puts it on an old garment; otherwise he will both tear the new, and the piece from the new will not match the old. And no one puts new wine into old wineskins; otherwise the new wine will burst the skins, and it will be spilled out, and the skins will be ruined (Luke 5:36-37).

The new cloth would tear the old cloth because it had not been "pre-shrunk." The old cloth had been washed many times and had already been shrunk. When the patch of new cloth was washed, it would shrink and tear the old cloth.

The new wine would burst the old wineskins during the fermenting stage. Old, brittle wineskins would not stretch. The pressure of the expanding new wine would cause the old wineskins to burst. New wineskins were soft and pliable and would expand with the fermenting wine.

The parable teaches two things about the "new" teachings of Jesus as they came into contact with the old religious practices of the Pharisees and the contemporary religious practices of the disciples of John the Baptist.

First, the teachings of Jesus must not be mixed with the religious practices of the traditional past or those of the contemporary culture. They are unique. They are not to be contaminated with other religions no matter how old and hallowed, no matter how new and trendy. Jesus said, "But new wine must be put into fresh wineskins" (Luke 5:38).

Second, people do not want to change their established religious practices. They have already "bought into" the system and consider change disruptive to their comfort zone and their pride. This must have been the thinking of the scribes of the Pharisees, for Jesus said, "And no one, after drinking old wine wishes for new; for he says, 'The old is good enough' " (Luke 5:39).

CULTURAL INFLUENCES ON WORSHIP

Every generation of Christians lives between the tensions of the traditional and the contemporary culture. The cultures are the same, only in different wrappings. Both stem from humanity and are not a part of God-commanded worship practices. This does not mean that either the traditional or the contemporary practices are themselves wrong. They might be neutral expedients of doing something commanded or taught by the Lord's authority.

Some people can remember many years ago that a white starched cloth covered the cup of grape juice and the plate of unleavened bread on the "communion table." Almost all congregations had this practice. It slowly passed away because people began to ask, "Why?" When it became evident that its purpose had been to keep flies out of the grape juice, and that flies were seldom a problem anymore, the cloth was removed. It was a practical tradition, an expedient to a command, that no longer had a use.

The "invitation song" is a time-honored tradition at the close of the sermon. Scripture authorizes singing but does not command a song after the sermon. The song is a practical tradition which began in the 19th century with evangelistic gospel meetings on the American frontier. A sermon asking people to obey Jesus Christ in faith, repentance and baptism needed some kind of a practical expedient to allow people to respond to this challenge. The song became a good tradition that is still very useful. It can, however, become a meaningless practice if singers disregard the opportunity or if sermons cease to be evangelistic. Then the problem is not with the invitation song but with the singers or the sermons.

Many other traditional practices are a part of congregational activities. Which song books to use, how to collect the contribution, how to order assembly worship and how long the preacher's sermon should be are all a part of human judgment traditions. We should not equate them with practices that come from the Scriptures.

Many traditional cultural practices have been "handed down" because of their practical use to expedite a teaching from the Lord. They are not bound, nor should they be. They should cease to exist when they no longer fulfill their original function.

Similarly, many traditional cultural practices are being "handed over" from the present culture. Like traditions from the past, they are of human origin.

They fall under the same critique as traditions from the past. First, are they a way to expedite a teaching of the Lord? Second, do they have a practical theological purpose? When the question "Why?" is asked, can we honestly answer that the proposed practice is better than the present practice? Third, is the new way so essential to the true worship of God that it becomes necessary to make a change even if we offend Christians who object?

God leaves the choice of song books, choice of devotional or Stamps-Baxter songs, order of the worship activities, position of the body when praying, use of an invitation song, use of table talks before the Lord's Supper and a multitude of other things to our judgment.

To judge, however, we must use several divine principles. First, whatever is done must be either a practice authorized by the Lord or something that expedites such a practice (Colossians 3:17). Singing is a command of the Lord, while song books are an expedient. Second, it must be proper and orderly (1 Corinthians 14:40). Third, it must edify others (v. 26). Fourth, it must not offend a fellow Christian, "for whom Christ died" (8:11).

Some practices absorbed from the contemporary religious culture and advocated by a number of churches of Christ do not fit these principles. One such practice is the divisive use of contemporary and traditional worship assemblies to accommodate generationally perceived needs. The problem is not in having different assemblies due to crowded conditions or work schedules.

The problem is using such assemblies to divide Christians along generational, cultural and temperamental lines.

Performance worship is another cultural perversion of worship. Some might object to the use of the word "performance." But whatever is advertised as a performance, looks and acts like a performance, is considered a performance by those involved, and is responded to as a performance, really is a performance.

This involves most solos, choirs, praise teams and other special music used to appeal to the secular society. The problem does not come from the number of persons singing, but from its nature as a performance to please people. The focus is on marketing to people rather than worshiping God. Jesus called those who prayed, gave alms and fasted in order to be honored by other people "hypocrites": "And when you pray, you are not to be as the hypocrites; for they love to stand and pray in the synagogues and on the street corners, in order to be seen by men. Truly I say to you, they have their reward in full" (Matthew 6:5).

Experiential-driven worship is another cultural perversion of worship. Feelings certainly are integral to worship, but feelings themselves are not worship. Pagan cults can stimulate the emotions and call it "god-in-ness," but such an experience has nothing to do with worshiping the only true God.

Female leadership in the assembly is another cultural perversion of worship. The Scriptures forbid it, but the culture demands it. Those who follow contemporary religious culture are seeking to push women into leadership roles as song leaders, prayer leaders, adult class teachers, pulpit preachers, deacons and elders. These practices conflict with the Scriptures and the practice of the early church (1 Corinthians 14:33-38).

The old error of using instrumental music in worship has raised its head in the church again. A number of congregations have already apostatized in this way. This apostasy has been helped along by what some regard as the innocent practice of singing with instrumental music either outside of the church building or inside the church building at times other than the Sunday morning assembly.

A classic example of assimilating worship to the culture resulting in division among God's people is the apostasy of Jeroboam. Jeroboam knew that if the two northern tribes continued to worship in Jerusalem he would lose his power. He said in his heart, "If this people go up to offer sacrifices in the house of the Lord at Jerusalem, then the heart of this people will return to their lord, even to Rehoboam king of Judah" (1 Kings 12:27).

He led an apostasy from God to retain his power. He changed the object of worship, the place of worship, the priesthood and the feast days according to what he "devised in his own heart." The 12 tribes worshiping together would unite the people. Worshiping separately would divide them. How the apostasy came about is recorded in Scripture:

> So the king consulted, and made two golden calves, and he said to them, "It is too much for you to go up to Jerusalem; behold your gods, O Israel, that brought you up from the land of Egypt." And he set one in Bethel, and the other he put in Dan. Now this thing became a sin, for the people went to worship before the one as far as Dan (1 Kings 12:28-30).

Jeroboam had a political motive in perverting the worship of Israel. He used assimilation with the culture to achieve his goal. The result: a divided Israel and the northern kingdom led into total apostasy. Note the pattern of this apostasy and others since. First, there was rejection of false worship. Soon, there was toleration of it in their midst. Next, there was an assimilation from the culture. Finally, the false worship was embraced and defended.

The devil has always used the change of divinely authorized worship to human counterfeits compatible to the culture as a tool to divide the God's people and lead them into apostasy.

QUESTIONS

1. Discuss the parable of the wineskins as it relates to:
   - Religious traditions of the past
   - Religious practices of the present
   - Practicing a religious ritual without a purpose

2. What are the differences between the "traditions of men" and "apostolic traditions?" (See Matthew 15:1-9 and 2 Thessalonians 2:15)
3. Name some religious traditions that had validity when they were started but now have lost their purpose.
4. Name ways a good tradition can become a bad tradition.
5. Discuss ways to discard empty, useless traditions from the past without offending those who wish to hold onto them.
6. How did compromising with the culture divide Israel and lead it into apostasy?

CHAPTER SIX

WORSHIP IN COMMUNITY

1 Corinthians 10:14-14:40

Worship can take place in a personal, private setting, a small group gathering or a formal assembly of the church. Scripture provides examples of all three:

• Personal, private setting – Jesus in Gethsemane (Matthew 26:36ff), Peter praying on the housetop (Acts 10:9) and the healing of Dorcas (9:36ff).

• Small-group gatherings – a prayer meeting in the house of Mary, the mother of Mark (Acts 12:12), Paul and Silas in the jail at Philippi (16:25) and Paul's tearful departure from the elders at Ephesus (20:36).

• Formal assembly of the church – the Antioch church being called together to receive a mission report from Paul and Barnabas (Acts 14:27), the Corinth church coming together to worship (1 Corinthians 11:18-20) and the church at Troas coming together to observe the Lord's Supper (Acts 20:7).

Four times Paul speaks of the assembled church in correcting the abuse of spiritual gifts: "If therefore the whole church should assemble together ... when you assemble, ... but if there is no interpreter, let him keep silent in the church; ... Let the women keep silent in the churches" (1 Corinthians 14:23, 26, 28, 34).

People worship in all kinds of environments and in all kinds of circumstances. Worship does not depend upon the number of people involved or the nature of their worship place.

Worship in Assembly

The most complete instructions found in the New Testament on worship were addressed to the church at Corinth. Confusion, disorder and a variety of worship errors infected the church. Paul's first letter to the church seeks to correct these problems. Note the following topics discussed in 1 Corinthians 10-14:

- Involvement with idolatry;
- Perverting the Lord's Supper;
- Disgraceful adornment of women when they prayed and prophesied;
- Pride and depression over the exercise of spiritual gifts;
- Refusing to understand that worship involved both spirit and mind;
- Refusing to make worship expressions edifying to those who heard;
- Allowing improper and disorderly conduct in their assemblies;
- Allowing spiritual leadership roles for women in the assembly.

These kinds of problems seemed to be a compromise with the pagan culture that surrounded them.

The Corinthian church had a problem with idolatry. Paul warned them about being associated with idolatry, as this contributed to the apostasy of Israel (1 Corinthians 10:7). He then showed them the incompatibility of participating in idol worship and observing the Lord's Supper: "You cannot drink the cup of the Lord and the cup of demons; you cannot partake of the table of the Lord and the table of demons" (1 Corinthians 10:21).

The Corinthian church had a problem with irrational worship practices. In discussing the abuse of the gift of tongues, Paul reminded them how they had come out of irrational pagan worship but were now reverting to it. Their irrational way of exercising the gift of tongues was similar to pagan ecstatic utterances. The practices were not identical, but they shared two traits: they were given without the prompting of the mind, and they could not be understood. Some used ecstatic utterances to impress those who came to the oracle at Delphi near Corinth. The abuse of the gift of tongues at Corinth had the appearance of pagan worship. At the beginning of his discussion of the abuse of spiritual gifts, Paul wrote: "You know that when you were pagans, you were led astray to the dumb idols, however you were led" (1 Corinthians 12:2).

The miraculous spiritual gift of speaking in foreign languages was immature, non-edifying and useless unless both the speaker and the listener understood it. Paul gave these regulations for the exercise of the gift of "tongues":

> Therefore let one who speaks in a tongue pray that he may interpret. For if I pray in a tongue, my spirit prays, but my mind is unfruitful. What is the outcome then? I shall pray with the spirit and I shall pray with the mind also; I shall sing with the spirit and I shall sing with the mind also (1 Corinthians 14:13-15).

Compromising Christian worship with idolatrous rituals and the experiential practices of the mystery religions brought disorder and confusion into the Christian assemblies. Paul rejected this cultural compromise with pagan worship.

Conduct in Community Worship

The Corinthian worship assemblies must have been something to witness. Some people would be speaking in foreign languages, and some would be prophesying "in the spirit." Women would be vocal and aggressive in leadership roles. No one really cared or understood what was going on. The church had excitement, confusion and disorder.

These activities were not worship, since it was not with the spirit and understanding (1 Corinthians 14:15). Neither the tongue speakers nor the listeners understood what was being said. Even if some knew the language, they probably could not understand because so many were speaking simultaneously.

It was not evangelistic. An unbeliever entering the assembly could not rationally understand what was going on and would be prompted to think, "These people must be mad" (1 Corinthians 14:23).

The activities were not edifying. The speakers got so caught up their actions that they did not care if they were edifying others. Paul gave this instruction: "[W]hen you assemble, each one has a psalm, has a teaching, has a revelation, has a tongue, has an interpretation. Let all things be done for edification" (1 Corinthians 14:26).

The activities were not authorized by God. Paul particularly focused on this in defining the role of women in the assembled church. He instructed them to be silent for four reasons.

First, it was not the custom of the churches for women to have spiritual leadership roles (1 Corinthians 14:33). Second, the law defined the role of women as, "let them subject themselves" (v. 34). Third, Paul himself affirmed that "it is improper for a woman to speak in church" (v. 35). Fourth, as the bottom line to all of this reasoning, Paul said this teaching came by the authority of Jesus: "If anyone thinks he is a prophet or spiritual, let him recognize that the things which I write to you are the Lord's commandment" (v. 37).

The women were told to "keep silent in the churches; for they are not permitted to speak" (1 Corinthians 14:34). They could speak to their husbands at home. They could participate in teaching with their husbands as Priscilla did with Aquila (Acts 18:26). They could teach their children and grandchildren as Lois and Eunice did Timothy (2 Timothy 1:5). They were instructed to teach the younger women (Titus 2:3-5). Yet, they were to be silent in the church.

There was and is a difference between even the general "submissive quietness" of a woman's role in God's order and the specific "silence" to be observed when "the whole church should assemble together" (1 Corinthians 14:23).

The silence of women in the Christian assembly was not a first-century cultural thing unrelated to our time. Women played a prominent leadership role in the pagan religion in both the Greek and Roman cultures but not so in the church. The church did not conform to the culture but was distinct from it. The teaching concerning the conduct of women in the assembled church came from the authority of the Lord and had nothing to do with the culture.

Paul gave the theological basis for this teaching in other places:

> For man does not originate from woman, but woman from man; for indeed man was not created for the woman's sake, but the woman for man's sake (1 Corinthians 11:8-9).

> For it was Adam who was first created, and then Eve. And it was not Adam who was deceived, but the woman being quite deceived, fell into transgression (1 Timothy 2:13-14).

Paul instructed those who were causing problems to stop talking and start listening. He told the ones speaking in tongues to keep silent in the church if no interpreter was present. Only two or three were to speak in the assembly even if there was an interpreter.

He told the prophesiers to keep silent if a revelation was given to another prophet. Only two or three were to prophesy in the assembly, one by one. If one of the prophets thought his message was so important that he had to keep on speaking, Paul said, "[T]he spirits of prophets are subject to prophets" (1 Corinthians 14:32). A speaker should not "hog the agenda."

Contrasting with the divisive, disorderly and unedifying assemblies at Corinth are the Christian assemblies described in extra-biblical literature. Pliny wrote to the Roman emperor, Trajan, to inform him about the conduct in the Christian assemblies:

> [T]hey were in the habit of meeting on a certain fixed day before it was light, when they sang in alternate verses a hymn to Christ, as to a god, and bound themselves by a solemn oath, not to any wicked deeds, but

never to commit any fraud, theft or adultery, never to falsify their word, nor deny a trust (Everett Ferguson, *Early Christians Speak*, p. 81).

How to Worship with Others

Worship must be done with the spirit and understanding; we use both will and mind. Worship must edify those who hear; listeners must understand and benefit from our words. Worship must be orderly; we should avoid confusion.

Paul emphasized these three major teachings about worship when the church assembled. When the church at Corinth disregarded these teachings, the following resulted:

- Meaningless worship. The Corinthians did not get anything out of their worship because it was not done with the spirit and understanding.

- Irrational confusion. They neither knew what they were saying nor understood what others were saying.

- A stumbling block. Their disorderly and unintelligible conduct appeared to be madness to an unbeliever.

- A lack of edification. Neither the ones speaking nor the ones hearing were edified. It was an exercise in spiritual futility.

Three verses in 1 Corinthians 14 summarize what needed to be done to correct the confusions.

The first verse deals with the source of worship. Worship comes from our spirit, our identity. We must desire to worship. Worship is more than going through the motions of cold, traditional worship rituals as a duty or a social expectancy. We must speak with understanding and mean what we say and do. As Paul wrote: "I shall pray with the spirit and I shall pray with the mind also; I shall sing with the spirit and I shall sing with the mind also" (1 Corinthians 14:15).

The second verse deals with one of the purposes of worship: "building up" others. Worship is not only vertical praise to God but also horizontal exhortation to others. We sing to "teach and admonish one another" (Colossians 3:16). We pray on behalf of "one another" (James 5:16). In observing the Lord's Supper, we should "wait for one another" (1 Corinthians 11:33).

Worshiping God cannot be separated from extending fellowship to His children. Jesus taught a person estranged from a fellow Christian needed to be reconciled before making an offering to God:

> If therefore you are presenting your offering at the altar, and there remember that your brother has something against you, leave your offering there before the altar, and go your way; first be reconciled to your brother, and then come and present your offering (Matthew 5:23-24).

Estrangement from a fellow Christian hinders our worship to God. This is evident in the way the Christians at Corinth had become divisive. They were so divided that they had even quit observing the Lord's Supper together. This worship perversion had serious spiritual consequences. Paul said, "For this reason many among you are weak and sick, and a number sleep" (1 Corinthians 11:30). They were coming together not for the better but for the worse because estrangement instead of exhortation lived in their hearts.

The writer of Hebrews discussed the Christian assembly to those discouraged Christians: "[L]et us consider how to stimulate one another to love and good deeds, not forsaking our own assembling together, as is the habit of some, but encouraging one another; and all the more, as you see the day drawing near" (Hebrews 10:24-25). Participation in the Christian assembly is a barometer indicating the genuineness of our commitment and the state of our spiritual maturity. In the assembly, we both edify and are edified. The Christian assembly is not a time to withdraw in emotional ecstasy or spiritual assertiveness. It is a time to build up our brothers and sisters, as Paul stressed: "Let all things be done for edification" (1 Corinthians 14:26).

The third verse deals with the kind of demeanor to be exercised in the Christian assembly. It is to be proper, decent and respectful. It is not a time to make light of the holy or to be crude and trivial with the divine.

The temple in Jerusalem was holy because God manifested His presence in the Holy Place. In the same way, the church is holy because it is God's temple, His dwelling place (1 Corinthians 3:16). Nothing stirred the anger of Jesus more in His personal ministry than the desecration of God's temple with secularism. He drove out the animals and overturned the tables of the moneychangers because it was not proper for them to be there (John 2:14-17). The church is God's holy temple today, and we should give it the same awesome respect Jesus had for the temple.

This is not to suggest that the meeting place of the church is sacred and can only be used for worship and Christian service. It is the church that is holy, not the place where Christians meet. At no time is this holiness of the church reflected more than when it is assembled.

Just as there was order in the worship of the tabernacle and the temple at Jerusalem, so should there be order in the Christian assembly. God expected the priest to do what He commanded in the way He commanded at the times He commanded. God's wrath fell upon Nadab and Abihu because they changed what God had decreed in tabernacle worship. What will be His judgment upon those who change what God has decreed in His church?

It is not wrong to change things used to expedite a Scriptural worship activity. For example, the change from "one cup" to "individual containers" did not depart from what God commanded. It was merely a cultural change done to expedite what God had commanded. We must not confuse the change in human traditional expedients with worship practices God has commanded. An expedient is not a command, but something with which a command is obeyed. A container to hold the fruit of the vine is an expedient in observing the Lord's Supper. It can be singular or plural, made of glass or plastic. The container only expedites obeying the command to partake of the fruit of the vine.

Change is neither good nor bad. It is inevitable. Change toward the will of God is restoration. Change away from the will of God is apostasy. When change is advocated in Christian worship, let's not resist it because it is different. It might bring us closer to God. But if change is for the sake of change, to draw attention to itself or to satisfy our human desires, we should resist it as a secular innovation. Paul said: "But let all things be done properly and in an orderly manner" (1 Corinthians 14:40).

The Christian assembly is more than a social gathering, a sacred duty or a religious good work. It has been decreed by the Lord Himself as a time of sweet communion with Him and others in God's family. It is a time to express the deep devotion of our inner spirit in praise and petitions and a time to exhort and admonish one another to "keep the faith." Worship is central to the Christian assembly.

QUESTIONS

1. What differences are there in personal, private worship, small group worship and assembly worship? As to practice? As to purpose?
2. What were the worship problems in the church at Corinth relating to idols? Relating to attitude?
3. What kind of conduct was bringing confusion and disorder to the Christian assembly at Corinth?
4. What instructions did Paul give to correct this conduct?
5. Explain these terms as relating to worship:
   - With the spirit and the understanding.
   - Let all things be done for edification.
   - Wait for one another.
   - Let all things be done in a proper and orderly manner.

CHAPTER SEVEN

DYNAMICS OF WORSHIP

Psalm 8:3-4; Matthew 6:1-18; John 4:23-24;
1 Corinthians 14:14-40; Revelation 4:11; 5:9-10

W e need to learn to worship with the correct external forms and meaningful words. External forms and religious words, however, are meaningless without inner spiritual devotion.

WHAT WORSHIP IS NOT

Worship is not witnessing an external performance to stimulate a mood of awe or create emotional excitement nor going through prescribed religious ceremonies to win the favor of God. No matter how beautiful the words, how awesome the surroundings or how accurate the ceremonial structure, God does not accept worship unless it comes from the spiritual part of man.

The location of worship need not be a holy mountain, a desert of solitude or even a richly adorned temple built in God's honor. Worship takes place inside us. Our attitude and motives must support and blend with all external acts of devotion.

If our religious motivations are traditional observances, social expectancy, duty or habit, we do not worship. We are only going through meaningless motions and saying empty words.

Worship is not a spectator sport in which the worshipers sit in the stands giving their approval or disapproval to those performing in the arena. In true worship, the worshipers are involved in the action. Worship is not a dramatic production in which the "clergy" are the actors and the worshipers are the audience. In true worship, God is the audience, and the worshipers are the actors.

God desires, but does not need, our worship. We are not doing God a favor to worship Him. This is the message of a song sung by Israel:

> O Israel, I will testify against you;
> I am God, your God. …
> I shall take no young bull out of your house,
> Nor male goats out of your folds.
> For every beast of the forest is Mine,
> The cattle on a thousand hills.
> I know every bird of the mountains,
> And everything that moves in the field is Mine.
> If I were hungry I would not tell you;
> For the world is Mine, and all it contains.
> Shall I eat the flesh of bulls,
> Or drink the blood of male goats?
> Offer to God a sacrifice of thanksgiving,
> And pay your vows to the Most High.
>
> (Psalm 50:7, 9-14)

Worship is not a dialogue between equals. We worship; God is the worshiped. Because of who He is, because of what He has done and is doing and will do, we worship Him. We prostrate our spirits in humility. We saturate our minds with praise and adoration. We fill our hearts with gratitude and glory. We can sing the song sung by the Israelites as they came to Jerusalem to worship:

> Shout joyfully to the Lord, all the earth.
> Serve the Lord with gladness;
> Come before Him with joyful singing.
> Know that the Lord Himself is God;

> It is He who has made us, and not we ourselves;
> We are His people and the sheep of His pasture.
>
> Enter His gates with thanksgiving,
> And His courts with praise.
> Give thanks to Him; bless His name.
> For the Lord is good;
> His lovingkindness is everlasting,
> And His faithfulness to all generations.
> (Psalm 100)

Worship is not a bargaining item to obtain the blessing of God. He cannot be bribed. Worship is not a duty to be performed as a legal requirement of law-keeping. If worship will not be motivated by love, it cannot be forced by law. Speaking with the tongues of men and of angels in worship is an empty noise without love (1 Corinthians 13:1).

Worship is not a psychological substitute for repentance. Religious exercises of generous giving, pious prayers and beautiful singing are not worship unless they come from a "broken and contrite heart" (Psalm 51:17). Worship is not merely group dynamics for social cohesion. Worship is not an "inward all-overness" better felt than told. Worship is not "word-only worship" no matter how accurate the ritual might be. Worship is not merely the 10 a.m. assembly at the church building.

The dynamics of true worship must have three essentials. First, true worship must have divine sanction. God has revealed how He wants to be worshiped, and we must not tinker with His desire. We would be just as wrong to change the God-authorized forms of worship as it we would to change the object of worship, God.

Second, true worship must come from the inner person as an expression of true devotion. Word-only worship does not please God. Jesus exposed this as false worship: "And when you are praying, do not use meaningless repetition, as the Gentiles do, for they suppose that they will be heard for their many words" (Matthew 6:7).

Third, true worship must satisfy the purposes for which it is given. Worship that does not emanate from our inner spirit is not true worship. Worship that does not praise God and edify others is not true worship.

WORSHIP PLEASING TO GOD

No matter how great our desire or how sincere our motive, God does not accept worship without divine sanction. Worship forms and patterns must be God-ordained.

No matter how noble our motive or how pious the ceremony, God does not accept ignorant worship. We do not question the sincerity or the pious motives of those who fall down before idols or of those who cut their bodies with knives in pseudo piety. Paul's message to idol worshipers who were "very religious in all respects" was for them to repent. He did not excuse their ignorance. He exposed their false worship by saying, "What therefore you worship in ignorance, this I proclaim to you" (Acts 17:23).

God does not accept worship following human traditions. The Pharisees criticized Jesus and His disciples because they did not keep the worship traditions handed down from the elders. There was the tradition of hand washing before eating bread (Matthew 15:2). There was the tradition of fasting which was observed both by the Pharisees and the disciples of John (Luke 5:33). Jesus clearly taught that binding human traditions conflicted with keeping the commandments of God. Mark recorded His teachings on traditions:

> Neglecting the commandment of God, you hold to the tradition of men. ... You nicely set aside the commandment of God in order to keep your tradition. ... thus invalidating the word of God by your tradition which you have handed down (Mark 7:8-9, 13).

God does not accept performance worship that seeks the favor of people. Jesus exposed the hypocrisy of those who performed acts of worship "to be seen of men." Performance worship can come in the form of a musical concert, a dramatic performance, a special contribution, an eloquent prayer or even a pious look designed to gain the approval of others. Worship that seeks the honor and praise of people is not acceptable worship (Matthew 6:1-18).

God does not accept arrogant worship. The very nature of worship is awesome, humble submission. Pride hinders worship. Jesus condemned the religious pride of the Pharisees and exposed their self-centeredness:

> But they do all their deeds to be noticed by men; for they broaden their phylacteries and lengthen the tassels of their garments. And they love the place of honor at banquets, and the chief seats in the synagogues, and respectful greetings in the market places, and being called by men, Rabbi (Matthew 23:5-7).

We can find an example of this kind of arrogant worship in one of Jesus' parables. He told of a Pharisee who prayed like this:

> God, I thank Thee that I am not like other people: swindlers, unjust, adulterers, or even like this tax-gatherer. I fast twice a week; I pay tithes of all that I get (Luke 18:11-12).

Jesus said that this man did not go home justified, because "everyone who exalts himself shall be humbled, but he who humbles himself shall be exalted" (Luke 18:14).

When God reveals the object of worship, it excludes everything else. The devil tempted Jesus and promised to give Him all the kingdoms of the world if He would fall down and worship him. Jesus responded by quoting from the law: "You shall worship the Lord your God, and serve Him only" (Matthew 4:10). Moses did not have to name all the so-called gods that have been and are worshiped by men. He affirmed who was to be worshiped and that excluded everything else.

When God reveals how a person should worship, He excludes everything else. Nadab and Abihu, the sons of Aaron, offered incense in the tabernacle after being instructed to take fire from the brazen altar for their firepans. They did not follow God's instructions; instead, they offered to God that which He "commanded not." Moses recorded the incident:

> Now Nadab and Abihu, the sons of Aaron, took their
> respective firepans, and after putting fire in them,
> placed incense on it and offered strange fire before the
> Lord, which He had not commanded them. And fire
> came out from the presence of the Lord and consumed
> them, and they died before the Lord (Leviticus 10:1-2;
> see also 16:12).

Worship must have God as the object. Worship must involve the right kind of offering. Worship must involved the right kind of attitude. Worship devised by human preference, cultural assimilation or human traditions does not please God.

Sources of Worship

The source of worship is just as important as the object and method of worship. Without the right source of worship, all religious ceremonies are empty and meaningless. We must not confuse stirring the emotions by external stimuli with worship. Worship is an inward expression, not an external impression. True worship includes understanding and subjective feelings, but its source is a willing spirit. We worship because we want to.

Sometimes the point of community worship is missed when people get so wrapped up in the incidental and forget the sources and purposes of worship. Sermon style and expedient structure are not the important thing; Paul preached until midnight. The style and the musical qualities of singing are not the important thing; Paul and Silas sang in a prison cell. The time, temperature and sound are not the important things. Worship must involve our head and heart as well as the right forms.

First, our spirit is involved in worship. Our spirit is our inner self, our identity, our volition or free will. The word translated "spirit" in the New Testament is *pneuma*. This word has more than one meaning. It can be translated "wind." Jesus used that meaning to describe the nature of the spirit. We can know it exists by hearing its sound, but its source and destination are unknown because it cannot be seen (John 3:8).

The source of our volition is our spirit. Our spirit is aware of our thoughts and wills us to act: "For who among men knows the thoughts of a man except the spirit of the man which is in him?" (1 Corinthians 2:11).

Worship takes place in the realm of the spirit, although there are external forms that reflect this spiritual reality. The God-authorized forms make this possible. God is spirit. Each of us has a spirit. We are, after all, created in His image! In this spiritual realm we have fellowship with God; in this spiritual realm worship takes place:

> But an hour is coming, and now is, when the true wor-
> shipers shall worship the Father in spirit and truth; for
> such people the Father seeks to be His worshipers.
> God is spirit, and those who worship Him must wor-
> ship in spirit and truth (John 4:23-24).

The spirit of a person, then, relates to God who is spirit in the realm of the spirit.

Second, our mind is involved in worship. Our mind is our rational, thinking, understanding self. Paul corrected the Corinthians' error of worshiping without understanding:

> For if I pray in a tongue, my spirit prays, but my mind
> is unfruitful. What is the outcome then? I shall pray
> with the spirit and I shall pray with the mind also; I
> shall sing with the spirit and I shall sing with the mind
> also. Otherwise if you bless in the spirit only, how will
> the one who fills the place of the ungifted say the
> "Amen" at your giving of thanks, since he does not
> know what you are saying? (1 Corinthians 14:14-16).

Corinthians speaking in a foreign language did not understand what they were saying; hence they were not worshiping. Those who heard did not understand what was being said; hence they could not say, "Amen." They might have been saying worship words in a devotional setting, but worship was not taking place. The words were mindless, meaningless utterances.

If we neglect to understand the words used in worship, we are not really worshiping. This holds true for both ecstatic utterances of charismatics and the mindless, memorized words of gospel songs sung in a congregational setting. The words spoken in worship must be understood by the mind and willed by the spirit.

Third, our heart is involved in worship. Our heart is our emotional, feeling part. It merges with our mind and spirit during true worship.

The threefold division of our being is not the only way to understand our nature. The Scriptures describe a person as "spirit and soul and body" (1 Thessalonians 5:23) and as "spirit and mind" (1 Corinthians 14:15). Sometimes the heart is used to describe our capacity to believe. Paul said, "[F]or with the heart man believes" (Romans 10:10). Sometimes the heart comes across as the emotional part, and sometimes it comes across as the rational part:

> speaking to one another in psalms and hymns and
> spiritual songs, singing and making melody with
> your heart to the Lord (Ephesians 5:19).

> The sacrifices of God are a broken spirit;
> A broken and a contrite heart, O God, Thou wilt
> not despise.
>   (Psalm 51:17)

> Let the words of my mouth and the meditation of
> my heart
> Be acceptable in Thy sight,
> O Lord, my rock and my Redeemer.
>   (Psalm 19:14)

Worship is more than the stirring of the emotions, but we cannot respond to God's love without being emotionally involved. Our spirit wills us to worship in awe before God's majesty. Our mind understands the words of praise and devotion. Our heart overflows with deep emotions.

Emotions can be stimulated and interpreted to be worship when the result is no more than a psychological phenomenon. Pagan ceremonies stimulate emotions. Drama stimulates the emotions. Music stimulates the emotions. Worship is "from the heart," but it must also be from the mind and spirit.

PURPOSES OF WORSHIP

True worship not only must be according to the teaching of the Scriptures and originate from our spirit, mind and heart, but it must also have the right purposes.

Worship is more than "a place to go" or a "ceremony to perform." It must have purpose. Without purpose, worship is an empty, meaningless exercise in futility.

The purpose of worship is, first of all, to express feelings from the depth of our soul. Sometimes our heart is so brimming with joy for God's blessings that we must pour it out in worship. This must have been the setting of a song composed by David:

> I will extol Thee, my God, O King;
> And I will bless Thy name forever and ever.
> Every day I will bless Thee,
> And I will praise Thy name forever and ever.
> Great is the Lord, and highly to be praised;
> And His greatness is unsearchable. ...
> On the glorious splendor of Thy majesty,
> And on Thy wonderful works, I will meditate.
> (Psalm 145:1-3, 5)

Sometimes our heart is so full of sorrow that it must be released in worship. Jesus went to Gethsemane and grew distressed and grieved. He wanted to worship in prayer. He told His disciples this:

> "My soul is deeply grieved, to the point of death; remain here and keep watch with Me." And He went a little beyond them, and fell on His face and prayed, saying, "My Father, if it is possible, let this cup pass from Me; yet not as I will, but as Thou wilt" (Matthew 26:38-39).

Luke recorded that His agony was so great and His prayer so fervent that "His sweat became like drops of blood, falling down upon the ground" (Luke 22:44).

Worship releases both joy and sorrow from the human heart. When we need to release deep emotions, worship comes naturally. James teaches that worship should be the Christian response to both joy and sorrow: "Is anyone among you suffering? Let him pray. Is anyone cheerful? Let him sing praises" (James 5:13).

A primary purpose of worship is to express deep feelings to God. A symphony or a dramatic production might stir and stimulate our emotions; these, however, are not worship. Worship is something we do, not something that is done to us.

Worship is an avenue for both giving praise and seeking aid. God responds, giving peace and contentment to the worshiper:

> Be anxious for nothing, but in everything by prayer
> and supplication with thanksgiving let your requests
> be made known to God. And the peace of God, which
> surpasses all comprehension, shall guard your hearts
> and your minds in Christ Jesus (Philippians 4:6-7).

Worship is the only thing we can give to God that is uniquely our own. God wants our worship. All of the pomp of ceremony, all of the orderliness of form, all of the beauty of art and all of the emotional stimulation evoked through drama and music cannot substitute for the simple devotion of one humble heart.

A second purpose of worship is to express praise to God. Christians do not offer animal sacrifices or burn incense in a temple as Israel did in Old Testament times. Our sacrifices are of a different nature. Instead of bulls and goats, Christians offer praise and thanksgiving: "Through Him then, let us continually offer up a sacrifice of praise to God, that is, the fruit of lips that give thanks to His name" (Hebrews 13:15).

When we come to realize just who God is, what He has done and how He loves us, praise flows naturally. Like the spiritual beings around the throne of God in heaven, we give praise to Him in awesome, humble submission. Revelation contains some of the songs sung by those who surround the throne of God and worship the Lamb:

> Holy, Holy, Holy, is the Lord God, the Almighty, who
> was and who is and who is to come (Revelation 4:8);

> Worthy art Thou, our Lord and our God, to receive glory and honor and power; for Thou didst create all things, and because of Thy will they existed, and were created (Revelation 4:11);

> Worthy art Thou to take the book, and to break its seals; for Thou wast slain, and didst purchase for God with Thy blood men from every tribe and tongue and people and nation (Revelation 5:9).

Because of the glory, the majesty, the power, the holiness and the nature of God, we worship. We stand in awe. We hide our face in humility. We fall before His presence in submission. He is God.

When Jesus made His triumphal entry into Jerusalem, a whole multitude began to praise God saying, "Blessed is the King who comes in the name of the Lord" (Luke 19:38). The Pharisees were displeased and asked Jesus to rebuke His disciples. Jesus said, "I tell you, if these become silent, the stones will cry out" (Luke 19:40). Praise is the natural response to the majesty of God.

Psalm 148 proclaims that all of creation praises Him since "He commanded and they were created" (v. 5). Revelation describes the angelic hosts and heavenly beings praising God around the heavenly throne. How much more should those of us redeemed by the blood of the Lamb and saved from the cup of wrath worship and praise Him!

A third purpose of worship is to edify others. There are times of private worship between a person and God. There are also times of public worship in the assembled church. It is in times of public worship that this third purpose of worship is needed. As discussed in the previous chapter, Paul needed to correct the confusion that existed in the assembled church at Corinth (1 Corinthians 14:23-40). Three solutions were needed to correct the confusion; the same solutions apply to us, too.

The first solution was to ensure that worship be understandable to both the leaders and followers. It must be understood by the one leading the worship in song and prayer. It must be understood by those who were following the words of the song and prayer. If the leader did not understand, he was not worshiping. If the followers did not understand, they could not reply, "Amen."

The second solution was to make worship edifying. Each word and deed should benefit those who hear and see. Worship acts should be conducted so that even an unbeliever will be benefited. Paul put it this way: "When you assemble, each one has a psalm, has a teaching, has a revelation, has a tongue, has an interpretation. Let all things be done for edification" (1 Corinthians 14:26).

Third, worship should be done "properly and in an orderly manner" (1 Corinthians 14:40). The Christian assembly at Corinth had several prophets speaking simultaneously. Paul instructed them to speak one at a time. If a revelation was given to a seated prophet, the speaking prophet was to keep silent.

Some in the assembly who had the gift of tongues were speaking without an interpreter. They were told to take turns and be silent if there was no interpreter.

Some of the women in the assembly were causing confusion by speaking out in a leadership role. Paul said that such conduct was contrary to the submissive role of women and because of that, they were to keep silent in the churches.

To worship in a proper and orderly way means that forethought should be given by the speaker as to when he is to speak and how long he is to speak. He should speak in a proper and orderly way so others can understand and be edified.

These solutions enhance worship for the lifelong church attendant as well as for someone visiting the church for the first time.

SUMMARY

A multitude of religious practices are called worship but fall short of what the Scriptures teach. Sadly, they are followed by devout and sincere people. These people's devotion and sincerity do not excuse their ignorance, though.

The object of worship is God. He alone is worthy of praise and awesome, humble submission in acts of worship. The sources of worship are our willing spirit, our thinking mind and our feeling heart. The purposes of worship are to express our deep emotions and devotion, to praise God because of His majestic glory and to edify others when worship is in community. The forms of worship are God-authorized, not human-devised. We must approach God in a spirit of awesome, humble submission in ways He has revealed. It is presumptuous to create other ways.

QUESTIONS

1. Name some misconceptions about what constitutes worship.
2. What is the threefold purpose of worship?
3. What is the threefold source of worship?
4. Why is it essential to have divine authority for worship forms?
5. What is wrong with the following:
   - Traditional worship?
   - Experiential worship?
   - Performance worship?
   - Arrogant worship?
6. Why must worship be decent and orderly?

SECTION TWO

WORSHIP PRACTICE

This section will give practical guidance in applying the biblical principles studied in the first section for personal and community worship. Worship should be practiced by the newest convert, but is something that even the most knowledgeable and experienced elder can better understand and practice.

Worship practices have been handed down by apostolic traditions. Paul complimented the Corinthians because they held "firmly to the traditions, just as [he] delivered them" (1 Corinthians 11:2). Paul told the church at Thessalonica, "[S]tand firm and hold to the traditions which you were taught, whether by word of mouth or by letter from us" (2 Thessalonians 2:15).

The next four chapters will discuss worship as it was given by apostolic authority and practiced in the New Testament church. Worship practices from cultural traditions of the past as well as from cultural assimilations from the contemporary culture are rejected because they do not have scriptural authority. Followers of Jesus must neither canonize the past nor mimic the present worship fads that are tied to the culture.

Each chapter also will provide suggestions on improving worship leadership and structure.

CHAPTER EIGHT

WORSHIP IN PRAISE AND PRAYER

Matthew 6:5-15; Romans 8:26;
1 Corinthians 14:15-16, 26; Ephesians 5:18-19;
Philippians 4:6-7; Colossians 3:16-17; James 5:13

Praise and prayer are combined in this chapter because they are similar in form and purpose. Paul joins singing and praying in discussing how worship emanates from both our spirit and understanding (1 Corinthians 14:15). James combines singing and praying in describing how worship arises from hearts filled with joy or sorrow (James 5:13). Both singing and praying consist of words of praise and thanksgiving. Both are directed to God. Both are to be given in such a way as to be understood in the assembly.

The acts can differ in at least two ways. First, worship words can be sung or spoken. Second, worship words can be spoken "to one another" in a group or spoken "by a leader," with the group giving an "amen" affirmation.

SINGING

Thirteen New Testament passages deal with singing. Two of them quote text from the Old Testament (Romans 15:9; Hebrews 2:12). Three are from apocalyptic literature (Revelation 5:9; 14:3; 15:3). Three are incidental references (Matthew 26:30; Mark 14:26; Acts 16:25).

Five passages relate to how we are to worship in song. Here are the first two: "I shall sing with the spirit and I shall sing with the mind also. ... When you assemble, each one has a psalm. ... Let all things be done for edification" (1 Corinthians 14:15, 26). The context of these two passages is Paul's correction of worship abuse at Corinth. Two points stand out in the passages – both spirit and mind are involved in worship in song, and everyone should understand and benefit from the songs in the assembly.

A third passage contrasts the irrational worship of Dionysus, the god of wine, with Christian worship in song.

> And do not get drunk with wine, for that is dissipation, but be filled with the Spirit, speaking to one another in psalms and hymns and spiritual songs, singing and making melody with your heart to the Lord (Ephesians 5:18-19).

Singing is for edification. It involves "speaking to one another." Singing is heartfelt praise to the Lord.

A fourth passage discusses the attributes a Christian should put on as a new self.

> Let the word of Christ richly dwell within you, with all wisdom teaching and admonishing one another with psalms and hymns and spiritual songs, singing with thankfulness in your heart to God (Colossians 3:16).

One attribute is gratitude to God. The passage also shows that singing can help us teach and admonish each another. It further shows that singing arises from a thankful heart.

A fifth passage is brief and expresses that singing praises is the natural expression of a cheerful heart: "Is anyone cheerful? Let him sing praises" (James 5:13).

Note from these passages that singing was done as personal praise to express joy, as edification to one another and as praise to the Lord. The text does not reveal the style of singing, the number of individuals doing the singing or whether there was a designated leader. The text merely mentions "singing." That excludes playing instruments of music, dancing and anything else we might want to add to worship in song. (For a fuller discussion of worship in song, see my book, *Worship in Song*.)

Worship in song should be given with a willing spirit, an understanding mind and a feeling heart. Its purposes are to express deep religious feelings, to edify those who hear and to praise God. We must worship in song as God has ordained in Scriptures without cluttering it with either the traditions of past cultures or the assimilations of the present culture. We must worship as God commanded and the apostles exemplified.

SUGGESTIONS FOR WORSHIP IN SONG

1. Singing praises is not a performance, a duty, a mindless ritual or a meaningless mumble. It should be understood as praise to the holy God and edification to brothers and sisters we love.

2. The congregation should all participate with both the spirit and understanding. This can be learned. A devout heart, an understanding mind and a willing spirit will seek to make the words of the mouth sincere and acceptable to God.

3. Singers should not focus on the musical sounds so much as on the worship taking place in everyone's heart.

4. True worshipers do not complain about the selection or style of the songs if they are scriptural and edifying. Diverse forms of singing – fast or slow, old hymns or new songs, four-part harmony or unison – are all acceptable even if they might not be everyone's preference.

5. The song leader should thoughtfully select songs in advance to ensure praise and edification. Both the content and the tempo of the songs can fit the sermon or a theme reflecting the needs of the congregation. He should also avoid calling attention to himself, the music or other things which might distract from worship.

Praying

Scripture mentions many teachings and examples of prayer, the expression of deep feelings to God. Prayer is an appropriate response to God in times of suffering and sorrow. Prayer can be for the sick. Prayer can be for the forgiveness of sins. James affirmed the privilege of prayer in times of need:

> Is anyone among you suffering? Let him pray. ... Is anyone among you sick? Let him call for the elders of the church, and let them pray over him. ... Therefore, confess your sins to one another, and pray for one another, so that you may be healed. The effective prayer of a righteous man can accomplish much (James 5:13-14, 16).

Prayer can also be an expression of praise and devotion. It can be thanksgiving for His care. We can pray about everything. Paul wrote, "Be anxious for nothing, but in everything by prayer and supplication with thanksgiving let your requests be made known to God" (Philippians 4:6).

Prayer can be a petition for one's needs and desires. It can be for wisdom to know how to respond to life's situations (James 1:5). It can be for rulers and those in authority. It can be for blessings for the beloved. It can even be for enemies (Matthew 5:44). Paul encouraged Christians to pray for everyone:

> First of all, then, I urge that entreaties and prayers, petitions and thanksgivings, be made on behalf of all men, for kings and all who are in authority, in order that we may lead a tranquil and quiet life in all godliness and dignity. ... I want the men in every place to pray, lifting up holy hands, without wrath and dissension (1 Timothy 2:1-2, 8).

The thought that "prayer moves the hand of Him who moves the world" is awesome! In every place, for everyone and about everything, we ought to pray.

All of divinity is involved in prayer. We address prayers to God the Father in the name of Jesus (Matthew 6:9; John 14:13-14).

The Holy Spirit helps when we do not know how to pray as we ought (Romans 8:26).

We offer prayers to God who "gives to all men generously and without reproach" (James 1:5). In His Sermon on the Mount, Jesus affirmed the effectiveness of prayer to the Father: "If you then, being evil, know how to give good gifts to your children, how much more shall your Father who is in heaven give what is good to those who ask Him!" (Matthew 7:11).

We offer prayers in the name of Jesus Christ. He is the One who became flesh and dwelt among men. He understands our plight, our temptations, our suffering and our fear of death. He sits on the right hand of the throne of God and is able to mediate for us:

> For we do not have a high priest who cannot sympathize with our weaknesses, but one who has been tempted in all things as we are, yet without sin. Let us therefore draw near with confidence to the throne of grace, that we may receive mercy and may find grace to help in time of need (Hebrews 4:15-16).

We offer prayers with the help of the Holy Spirit. Paul taught that the Spirit of God knows the mind of God (1 Corinthians 2:11). It is this same Holy Spirit that we receive when we are baptized for the remission of sins (Acts 2:38). The Holy Spirit becomes the communication connector when we pray. This is a work of the Holy Spirit that transcends what He does through the Word of God:

> And in the same way the Spirit also helps our weakness; for we do not know how to pray as we should, but the Spirit Himself intercedes for us with groanings too deep for words; and He who searches the hearts knows what the mind of the Spirit is, because He intercedes for the saints according to the will of God (Romans 8:26-27).

The Father, the Son and the Holy Spirit are all involved in the prayers we offer to God. This should give us a sense of awe in our praise and a sense of confidence in our petitions. God greatly desires our worship and has provided a way to come into His majestic presence in praise and prayer.

We must avoid some types of prayer, though. The right form and the right words mean nothing if the foundation is faulty.

A proud prayer is ineffective. Jesus condemned the Pharisee who boasted to God with these words: "God, I thank Thee that I am not like other people: swindlers, unjust, adulterers, or even like this tax-gatherer. I fast twice a week; I pay tithes of all that I get" (Luke 18:11-12). Jesus said the man who offered such a prayer was not justified, "for everyone who exalts himself shall be humbled."

A ritual prayer is ineffective. We might say religious words with a pious voice and in a religious place, but if they do not come from our heart, they will not please God. Someone has written, "I might as well bow down and worship gods of stone as offer to a living God a prayer of words alone." Jesus quoted Isaiah and said, "This people honors Me with their lips, but their heart is far away from Me. But in vain do they worship Me" (Matthew 15:8-9).

A performance prayer is ineffective. It, like all performance, is directed to the audience. It is done to be seen of others. Jesus called those who practiced such pretended piety "hypocrites": "And when you pray, you are not to be as the hypocrites; for they love to stand and pray in the synagogues and on the street corners, in order to be seen by men. Truly I say to you, they have their reward in full" (Matthew 6:5).

A doubter's prayer is ineffective. To ask God for something that we do not believe He will answer is folly, an exercise in futility. A person who prays a prayer of doubt is "double-minded" and "unstable in all his ways." James wrote, "But let him ask in faith without any doubting, for the one who doubts is like the surf of the sea driven and tossed by the wind. For let not that man expect that he will receive anything from the Lord" (James 1:6-7).

A selfish prayer is ineffective. When we pray, we should include our "thank you's" along with our "give me's." Maybe our prayers should not be so much, "Give me things to make me happy," but rather, "Help me to be happy with the things You give." James condemned selfish prayers: "You ask and do not receive, because you ask with wrong motives, so that you may spend it on your pleasures" (James 4:3).

A willful prayer is ineffective. It is significant that when Jesus prayed in the garden that "this cup might pass from [Him]," He ended His prayer with, "Father, if Thou art willing, remove this cup from Me; yet not My will, but Thine be done" (Luke 22:42). He desired the cup of wrath pass from Him, but His first priority was that the will of God be done. John wrote of the importance of praying according to the will of God:

> And this is the confidence which we have before Him, that, if we ask anything according to His will, He hears us. And if we know that He hears us in whatever we ask, we know that we have the requests which we have asked from Him (1 John 5:14-15).

A prayer from a disobedient person is ineffective. Even though it was an uninspired man who said, "We know that God does not hear sinners; but if any one is God-fearing, and does His will, He hears him" (John 9:31), he was right. Certainly God hears and knows everything. Certainly God is responsive to the prayers of pious people like Cornelius. Understand, however, that God does not respond to the prayers of those who disobey him in the same way He does to those who obey Him: "[W]hatever we ask we receive from Him, because we keep His commandments and do the things that are pleasing in His sight" (1 John 3:22).

A neglected prayer is ineffective. If we do not ask, we will not receive. If we do not seek, we will not find. If we do not knock, a door will not be opened. We can rob ourselves of great blessings by merely seeking to accomplish goals on our own without asking for the blessing of God. James wrote, "You do not have because you do not ask" (James 4:2). Instead of trying to "go it on our own," we should say, "If the Lord wills, we shall live and also do this or that" (James 4:15).

SUGGESTIONS FOR WORSHIP IN PRAYER

1. Think about what you need and want to pray about. Consider everything that falls under your concern. Prayer is not a shopping list, but our every concern is God's concern. Sometimes a list – written down or updated on a computer – is helpful.

2. Begin the prayer with praise. Do not be too concerned with the beauty of the words; the Holy Spirit will interpret the thoughts of the heart when we know not how to pray.

3. Include many thanksgivings in your prayer. As the song exhorts, "Count your blessings, name them one by one and it will surprise you what the Lord has done."

4. If you are leading in a prayer for a group:

   a. Consider their needs as well as your own. They are praying with you and should be able vocally or mentally to give an "amen" affirmation to what you say.

   b. Speak loudly and in language that everyone can understand. One prays to God, not the audience, but they cannot pray for what they do not hear and understand.

   c. Have an attitude of awe, humility and submission. Prayer must not be a performance, a duty or a mindless ritual of meaningless mumbling. It should glorify God and edify the brothers and sisters we love.

WORSHIP IN SONG AND PRAYER

Singing and praying fit the purposes of worship discussed in Chapter 6. They express the deep feelings of the soul. Singing, for example, is often involved in weddings to express joy and in funerals to express sorrow. After Jesus instituted the Lord's Supper in the Upper Room, He sang a hymn with His disciples. After being beaten at Philippi and having their feet in stocks in the inner prison, Paul and Silas sang hymns of praise to God. Prayer offers relief to the suffering and provides release to the cheerful.

While primarily directed to God, singing and praying also edify others. Singing is "speaking to one another" in song. One of its purposes is to "teach and admonish." When singing or praying is done in community, more is involved than one person communing with God. Other worshipers are also involved. They must hear and understand. When we sing a psalm, it must edify. When we offer a prayer, the hearers must understand if they are to give an "amen."

Physical Posture

The Scriptures do not give a specific physical position we are to assume in worshiping. This, like the place of worship, is incidental. We can stand with upturned faces. We can bow our face. We can kneel. We can raise our hands. We can close our eyes. We can sit with our feet trapped in stocks.

Two criteria should govern the physical position in worship. First, it should be the genuine, natural expression of the heart, not merely mimicking the fads of the past or present culture. Second, it should not be offensive to other people with whom you are worshiping.

Singing and praying offer praise and petitions to God. Singing is to be "with the heart" and "to the Lord" (Ephesians 5:19). They are to be "with thankfulness in your hearts to God" (Colossians 3:16). Jesus in His model prayer taught His disciples to offer praise and petitions: "Our Father who art in heaven, Hallowed be Thy name. … Give us this day our daily bread. And forgive us our debts, as we also have forgiven our debtors. And do not lead us into temptation, but deliver us from evil" (Matthew 6:9, 11-13).

Singing and praying are the two acts of worship in which heartfelt words of praise and petitions are directed to God. They may be done either in public or private at any time or place. They are the Christian sacrifice: "Through Him then, let us continually offer up a sacrifice of praise to God, that is, the fruit of lips that give thanks to His name" (Hebrews 13:15).

Questions

1. How are singing and praying similar? How are they different?
2. What function do God, Jesus and the Holy Spirit have in responding to our prayers?
3. For what should people pray?
4. What is the purpose of singing?
5. What hinders our prayers from being answered?
6. Name some factors which should be included in a congregational prayer.

CHAPTER NINE

WORSHIP IN THE LORD'S SUPPER

Matthew 26:26-29; Mark 14:22-25;
Luke 22:17-20; Acts 20:7; 1 Corinthians 10:16-21; 11:17-34

A central part of Christian worship is observing the Lord's Supper when the church meets on the first day of the week. The Lord's Supper is a memorial of the defining event of our faith, the death of Jesus Christ. It also proclaims the triumphant hope of the return of the Lord. In its observance, the church communes with Jesus and with one another in a sacred messianic meal. Unlike singing and praying, the Lord's Supper takes place at a certain time and place – on the first day of the week and in the assembly of Christians.

The practice of worship in the Lord's Supper has been perverted. Some claim that the bread and grape juice become the literal body and blood of Jesus by a miracle. Some deviate from the apostolic practice of observing it on the first day of the week and partake of it at times of their own discretion. Some make it a meaningless ritual by observing only the form without experiencing internal worship. Some trivialize it so much that they observe it quarterly, annually or just on special occasions.

Layers of human traditions have diverted the real focus of the Lord's Supper in some places. The tradition of using a white cloth to cover the bread and grape juice is now rarely seen because the need to keep flies away no longer exists. The tradition of all drinking from one cup is now rarely seen because smaller and more sanitary cups are available. The tradition of using wine instead of unfermented grape juice is now rarely seen because of the ability to preserve grape juice without the fermenting process taking place. None of these human traditions are wrong within themselves. They were solutions to practical problems. They only become wrong when the traditions not found in Scripture are forced upon others.

ITS ORIGIN

Jesus instituted the Lord's Supper at the end of the Passover feast of the Jews. He told His disciples what it meant, what elements were to be used and how it was to be done.

The Passover meal was a Jewish memorial meal to remember the Exodus from Egypt. An important part of the feast was the Passover lamb which was killed and eaten by everyone in every household. Before the Exodus, Israelites placed the blood of the slain lamb on their doorposts. This act saved the Israelites from the plague of death that came upon the firstborn in all of Egypt.

The Passover feast of the Jews is not the same thing as the Lord's Supper Jesus gave to His disciples, but the symbolism is similar. Both memorial feasts focus on the most significant event of their respective histories. Both center upon a bloody sacrifice. The Jews had the blood of the Passover lamb that saved them from death in Egypt. Christians have the blood of Jesus that saves them from sin and its penalty. Jesus connected the symbolism when He said, "I have earnestly desired to eat this Passover with you before I suffer; for I say to you, I shall never again eat it until it is fulfilled in the kingdom of God" (Luke 22:15-16). Through this memorial meal they could remember His crucified body and His shed blood. Through this messianic banquet He would commune with them in the kingdom soon to be established.

The elements of the Lord's Supper were unleavened bread and the fruit of the vine, items used in the Passover meal. The bread was unleavened to remember that the Exodus happened rapidly, not allowing time for leaven to make the bread rise. The grape juice was no doubt fermented wine as there was no way to preserve grape juice without fermentation. Both were excellent symbols to represent the body and blood of Jesus. Other kinds of food were on the Passover table, such as roasted lamb and bitter herbs, but Jesus chose unleavened bread and the fruit of the vine. It is the sin of presumption to change what Jesus chose.

Jesus gave thanks and then gave it to His disciples. Of the bread, He said, "Take, eat; this is My body." Of the fruit of the vine, he said, "Drink from it, all of you." (Matthew 26:26-27) They ate of the same bread and drank of the same cup. The communal meal bound them together as one body.

Jesus told the disciples that this was not the last time and place in which He would observe this memorial feast with them. He said, "But I say to you, I will not drink of this fruit of the vine from now on until that day when I drink it new with you in My Father's kingdom" (Matthew 26:29). Jesus promised that He would be present when they – and we would observe the Lord's Supper. He communes with His disciples in the "kingdom of God," the church Jesus promised to establish (Matthew 16:18-19). The Lord's Supper allows us to enjoy table fellowship with the King of Kings and the Lord of Lords.

ITS ABUSE

In correcting the Corinthian Christians who were participating in idolatrous worship, Paul showed worshiping in the Lord's Supper as an exclusive communion with the Lord:

> Is not the cup of blessing which we bless a sharing in the blood of Christ? Is not the bread which we break a sharing in the body of Christ? ... You cannot drink the cup of the Lord and the cup of demons; you cannot partake of the table of the Lord and the table of demons (1 Corinthians 10:16, 21).

The Lord's Supper joins the Christian in a communion with Christ. The Greek *koinonia* means "sharing" and is also translated as "communion," "participation" and "fellowship."

To worship a false god or to worship in a false way compromises one's relationship with Christ. Christ and idols are incompatible. So are participating in idol worship and worshiping the Lord. Worshiping anyone or anything besides God or employing worship practices not originating from God would be contaminating compromises.

With worship, we engage in more than a social activity or a cultural custom. We become a part of whom or what we worship. This is especially true in the Lord's Supper. Paul described this fellowship of the body: "Since there is one bread, we who are many are one body; for we all partake of the one bread" (1 Corinthians 10:17).

He added that this also applied to the sacrifices offered in the temple and the sacrifices offered to idols. Worshipers become a part of what they worship and with whom they worship. By participating in false worship to a false god, worshipers not only tolerate those with whom they differ religiously; but also approve and sanction what is contrary to the will of God. Paul wrote:

> Look at the nation Israel; are not those who eat the sacrifices sharers in the altar? ... [T]he things which the Gentiles sacrifice, they sacrifice to demons, and not to God; and I do not want you to become sharers in demons. You cannot drink the cup of the Lord and the cup of demons; you cannot partake of the table of the Lord and the table of demons (1 Corinthians 10:18, 20-21).

THE PATTERN

Paul's instructions in 1 Corinthians 11:17-34 give the fullest teaching in the Scriptures on worshiping in the Lord's Supper. The Corinthian Christians did not seem to be following the apostolic tradition of observing the Lord's Supper. They had been holding firm to some traditions that had been delivered to them, and Paul praised them for this (11:2). But in regard to the Lord's Supper, he said:

> I do not praise you, because you come together not for
> the better but for the worse. For, in the first place, when
> you come together as a church, I hear that divisions
> exist among you; and in part I believe it. ... Therefore
> when you meet together, it is not to eat the Lord's
> Supper (1 Corinthians 11:17-18, 20).

Paul implied that when they came together it should be to
observe the Lord's Supper. Later in the same letter he wrote of
their custom of coming together on the first day of the week
(1 Corinthians 16:1-2). This would imply that they were observing the Lord's Supper on the first day of the week. This seemed
to be the approved apostolic practice. Luke noted, "And on the
first day of the week, when we were gathered together to break
bread, Paul began talking to them" (Acts 20:7).

The consensus of early church history confirms this practice.
No evidence exists, in either the Scriptures or early church history, challenging the practice of Christians meeting together on
the first day of the week to observe this sacred meal.

Factions and divisions existed in the Corinthian church, so much
so that the Christians were worshiping in different groups when
they took the Lord's Supper. Paul instructed them, "[W]hen you
come together to eat, wait for one another" (1 Corinthians 11:33).

We do not know why the different groups chose to worship
separately, but the choice was wrong because it was motivated
by divisiveness. It could have been due to the preacher party factions mentioned in chapters one and three. It could have been
tensions between social, economic or ethnic groups. It could even
have involved generational differences or temperamental preferences like what is currently known as "Vietnam baby boomers"
versus "World War II builders" or even the "right brain" versus
"left brain" personalities. The error was not in meeting at different times because of space or schedules. It was because of
their exclusiveness and party spirit.

Corinth was becoming a weak, sick and dead church. The problems it had with idol worship, neglecting to follow apostolic traditions and becoming divisive in observing the Lord's Supper

were drawing all the spiritual life out of them. Their Lord's Supper actions intermingled with the others. Paul predicted these consequences would result from their worship perversion: "For he who eats and drinks, eats and drinks judgment to himself, if he does not judge the body rightly. For this reason many among you are weak and sick, and a number sleep" (1 Corinthians 11:29-30).

The phrase "judge the body rightly" can be understood in different ways. It can refer to remembering the physical body of Jesus on the cross, or it can refer to the body of Christ, the church. Both are true. Here, apparently, Paul was referring to the divisiveness in the church that was causing some to be weak and sickly and others to die spiritually. Factions in the church are unhealthy; if left uncorrected, they cause spiritual sickness and death among its members.

DEFINING THE LORD'S SUPPER

Paul sought to correct the different abuses of the Lord's Supper by defining it in seven ways. If Christians emphasize its true meaning and the right way to observe it, they can correct many of the corrupting errors.

First, the Lord's Supper is a sacred tradition. Paul had delivered this tradition to them, and he did not praise them for the way they were neglecting to follow it. The phrases "I received" and "I delivered" show that this tradition was apostolic and came from the Lord: "I received from the Lord that which I also delivered to you" (1 Corinthians 11:23).

Traditions are either good or bad depending on their source. Human traditions are not religious authority. Traditions from Jesus and the apostles are.

Second, the Lord's Supper is a messianic banquet. Jesus promised His disciples when He instituted the Lord's Supper that He would eat and drink it with them in His kingdom (Luke 22:18). Every first day of the week, the citizens of His kingdom gather around the table of the Lord to eat the bread and drink the fruit of the vine. Every time, Jesus the host is present. It is a time of sacred communion with Jesus and His church. Christians share in the eating of one loaf and drinking of one cup. They share the memory of the death of Jesus and the hope of His coming again. The assembly is not only a place of community edification involving singing, praying, teaching and giving; it is also a set time of remembering the sacrificial body and blood of Jesus on the cross. The strength in the assembly is shown in Jesus' teachings: "For where two or three have gathered together in My name, there I am in their midst" (Matthew 18:20).

Third, the Lord's Supper is a thanksgiving feast. Both in Paul's description of the Lord's Supper and in Matthew's and Luke's accounts of its origin, the text says that Jesus "gave thanks" before giving the bread to the disciples. The Greek word is *eucharistesas* from which we get the English word "eucharist." Although Jesus used the word in blessing the bread, His disciples can use the word in referring to thanksgiving to God for sending His Son and to Jesus for giving His life. In the Lord's Supper we can give thanks to God for so much.

Fourth, the Lord's Supper is a memorial supper. Jesus told His disciples, "Do this in remembrance of Me." America has a national holiday during which citizens remember those who have sacrificed so much –"Memorial Day." Every first day of the week is a memorial day for Christians. We remember Jesus' sacrifice on the cross and the blood He shed for our sins. Our remembrance of Jesus does not focus on a monument, a building or a location. It focuses on a supper in which we have a personal, spiritual communion with Him.

Fifth, the Lord's Supper is a covenant meal. When Jesus died upon the cross, the Old Covenant was nullified. With the shedding of His blood, the New Covenant was put in force. The conditions of a covenant are ratified with the shedding of blood. Hebrews speaks of the covenant God made with Israel:

> For when every commandment had been spoken by Moses to all the people according to the Law, he took the blood of the calves and the goats, with water and scarlet wool and hyssop, and sprinkled both the book itself and all the people, saying, "This is the

blood of the covenant which God commanded you"
(Hebrews 9:19-20).

The new covenant was established with the blood of Jesus.
When He instituted the Lord's Supper, He gave the cup and said
to His disciples, "[T]his is My blood of the covenant, which is
poured out for many for forgiveness of sins" (Matthew 26:28).
We should not observe this covenant meal, made holy by the
blood of Jesus Christ, lightly or frivolously.

Sixth, the Lord's Supper is a proclamation celebration. When
something of great significance is going to happen, a celebration
dinner is often planned to announce it. An engaged couple holds
a dinner to announce their plans to marry. A university hosts
an announcement dinner to proclaim a major gift to the school.
The Lord's Supper is a proclamation to celebrate the victory Jesus
had over the devil in His resurrection. Paul said, "For as often as
you eat this bread and drink the cup, you proclaim the Lord's
death until He comes" (1 Corinthians 11:26). On every first day
of the week, disciples of Jesus Christ proclaim to the world not
only that He died for its sins, but also that He is coming again to
judge it. This purpose of the Lord's Supper is perverted by those
who change the Lord's Supper assembly to Wednesday so as not
to make "seekers" uncomfortable.

Seventh, the Lord's Supper is a family fellowship. It is probably this aspect of the Lord's Supper that Paul was wanting to emphasize to the Corinthians. All of God's children are brothers and
sisters and should be treated as such. Exclusiveness in observing the Lord's Supper was playing havoc with the Corinthian fellowship. It could well have been this unbrotherly conduct that
prompted Paul to say:

> Therefore whoever eats the bread or drinks the cup of
> the Lord in an unworthy manner, shall be guilty of the
> body and the blood of the Lord. ... For he who eats and
> drinks, eats and drinks judgment to himself, if he does
> not judge the body rightly (1 Corinthians 11:27, 29).

Jesus gave a similar teaching about the priority of making things
right with a fellow Christian before approaching God in worship:

> If therefore you are presenting your offering at the altar, and there remember that your brother has something against you, leave your offering there before the altar, and go your way; first be reconciled to your brother, and then come and present your offering (Matthew 5:23-24).

We hinder worship when we are estranged from a brother or sister. We handicap spiritual growth if we refuse to observe the Lord's Supper with fellow Christians because of mere cultural preferences. When this happens, open division lurks nearby.

Understanding the noble purposes of the Lord's Supper and the way Paul described it by different analogies makes worship in the Lord's Supper very significant. It is a central part of the Christian assembly and a sacred act in which we join with Jesus and one another in a Messianic memorial feast.

SUGGESTIONS FOR WORSHIP IN THE LORD'S SUPPER

1. Serving of the Lord's Supper is an orderly process. Those who lead in prayer and serve should be chosen early and informed about where they will serve and how they will handle the trays.

2. Those who lead prayers for the cup and loaf should be either experienced or guided in the use of appropriate language. A midweek class can instruct men for this purpose.

3. "Table Talks" are very good in educating and focusing the congregation on the purpose and the meaning of the Lord's Supper. These talks should be scriptural, sharply focused and brief. Humor, personal experiences and unnecessary changes detract from the sanctity of the occasion. One of Paul's sevenfold descriptions of the Lord's Supper given above could very well form the basis of a "table talk."

Some appropriate passages for table talks include:

- 1 Corinthians 10:16-21
- 1 Corinthians 11:23-26
- Mark 14:22-25
- Matthew 27:33-37, 45-46, 50-54
- Luke 23:33-38, 44-46
- Mark 15:22-26, 33-34, 37-39
- 1 Corinthians 11:17-21
- Matthew 26:26-30
- Luke 22:17-20
- Acts 20:7
- John 19:23-30
- Isaiah 53:1-6

4. A song focusing on the Crucifixion before serving the Lord's Supper can help the congregation focus on its purpose.

5. Pageantry, drama and ceremonial trappings all detract from the simplicity of worship in the Lord's Supper.

6. The most important suggestion: We as worshipers need to discipline our thoughts upon the greatest event in all of history, the incarnate God dying on a cross to atone for our sins.

SUMMARY

The Lord's Supper was instituted by Jesus Himself before His crucifixion. He told His disciples that He would observe it anew with them at a certain time in His kingdom. It was to be a memorial feast eaten together with Jesus and His disciples until He came again. The elements of unleavened bread and fruit of the vine were used by Jesus.

The Lord's Supper was perverted by some in the church at Corinth. Apparently, it was combined with the "love feast." We know that it became an expression of divisiveness since it was not observed together by the whole church. This perversion rendered the church weak, sickly and in danger of dying.

Paul responded to the perversion of the Lord's Supper by giving the most complete account of how it was to be observed. This account, Paul said, he received from the Lord and was delivering it to the church at Corinth as a pattern.

QUESTIONS

1. Compare the similarities and differences of the Lord's Supper and the Passover feast of the Jews.
2. What elements are used in the Lord's Supper? What do they symbolize?
3. Discuss each of the seven ways Paul describes the Lord's Supper to the Corinthians.
4. How were the Corinthians abusing the Lord's Supper?
5. When is the Lord's Supper to be observed?
6. How can observing the Lord's Supper be improved?

CHAPTER TEN

WORSHIP
IN GIVING

Acts 11:27-30; Romans 15:25-27;
1 Corinthians 16:1-4; 2 Corinthians 8-9

Giving may be called an act of worship because it involves the threefold purposes of worship. First, worship is the expression of the inner, spiritual part of man. Giving fits this purpose. Paul commended the Macedonians for their spirit of generosity: "For I testify that according to their ability, and beyond their ability, they gave of their own accord. ... [A]nd this, not as we had expected, but they first gave themselves to the Lord and to us by the will of God" (2 Corinthians 8:3, 5). They gave "of their own accord" and "first gave themselves."

The giving involved an act of the will and the expression of generosity of the inner man. Paul focused on this aspect of giving in motivating the Corinthians to give from the heart: "Let each one do just as he has purposed in his heart; not grudgingly or under compulsion; for God loves a cheerful giver" (2 Corinthians 9:7).

Second, worship is directed to God. The Macedonians directed their giving to God. They "gave themselves to the Lord." Jesus taught that giving to needy children of God, His brothers, was in reality giving to Him: "Truly I say to you, to the extent that you did it to one of these brothers of Mine, even the least of them, you did it to Me" (Matthew 25:40).

Giving to those in need is motivated by more than sympathy for their plight. It is an act of mercy which is given to the Lord for the benefit of His brothers and sisters. Helping a needy Christian cannot be separated from love for God:

> We know love by this, that He laid down His life for us; and we ought to lay down our lives for the brethren. But whoever has the world's goods, and sees his brother in need and closes his heart against him, how does the love of God abide in him? (1 John 3:16-17).

Giving is a command of God and was a practice of the early church. Paul instructed the Corinthians how to give:

> Now concerning the collection for the saints, as I directed the churches of Galatia, so do you also. On the first day of every week let each one of you put aside and save, as he may prosper, that no collections be made when I come (1 Corinthians 16:1-2).

Everyone was to give, on the first day of every week, according to individual prosperity.

Third, worship in community should edify others. The giving of the Macedonians was for the benefit of the poor in Jerusalem. Paul spoke of their gift in his letter to Rome: "For Macedonia and Achaia have been pleased to make a contribution for the poor among the saints in Jerusalem" (Romans 15:26). Their gift was from the heart, to God and for needy saints at Jerusalem. The fulfillment of these purposes of worship allow us to call giving an act of worship.

As already shown, the words translated "worship" convey two ideas: a sense of awe and humble submission as well as formal acts of religious service. Giving involves both. It involves a personal commitment to the Lord to give as we prosper and "purpose in our heart" to perform acts of benevolence and preach the Gospel to the lost.

Hebrews connects "sharing" or giving with other acts of worship such as praise and thanksgiving: "Through Him then, let us continually offer up a sacrifice of praise to God, that is, the fruit of lips that give thanks to His name. And do not neglect doing good and sharing; for with such sacrifices God is pleased" (Hebrews 13:15-16). The Jews offered sacrifices of animals for worship at the temple. Christians offer sacrifices of praise and sharing for worship in the church.

INNER MOTIVES FOR GIVING

The inner motives of the heart must be right before God accepts our worship. Jesus condemned the Pharisees because they gave external, word-only worship without heartfelt motivation: "This people honors Me with their lips, but their heart is far away from Me. But in vain do they worship Me, teaching as doctrines the precepts of men" (Matthew 15:8-9).

Giving, as worship, is more than dropping a check in the contribution plate or fulfilling a pledge you have made to the church. It must be an expression of piety, compassion and love arising from the inner spirit of a person.

Giving is more than a duty we have to perform to make a payment on the building or buy more song books. Wanting to respond to an announcement from the pulpit about meeting a certain need is fine, but that must not be the primary motive of giving. Paul taught this to the Corinthians. A real need existed among the poor saints in Jerusalem. The churches in Achaia had planned and promised to help. The time had come for them to come through with the needed funds. Paul wanted them to give, but not as duty. He said that their giving should not be "grudgingly or under compulsion; for God loves a cheerful giver" (2 Corinthians 9:7).

Giving is more than for show. Jesus condemned false piety:

> Beware of practicing your righteousness before men to be noticed by them; otherwise you have no reward with your Father who is in heaven. When therefore you give alms, do not sound a trumpet before you, as

the hypocrites do in the synagogues and in the streets,
that they may be honored by men. Truly I say to you,
they have their reward in full (Matthew 6:1-2).

Jesus used an easy-to-remember statement to show the importance of secret giving: "[D]o not let your left hand know what you right hand is doing" (Matthew 6:3).

Giving is not bribing God to gain His favor. God's favor is not for sale. God does not need our actions or gifts. It is foolish to think we can merit His blessings:

> For every beast of the forest is Mine,
> The cattle on a thousand hills.
> I know every bird of the mountains,
> And everything that moves in the field is Mine.
> If I were hungry, I would not tell you;
> For the world is Mine, and all it contains.
>   (Psalm 50:10-12)

God does reward those who give according to His will, but not necessarily by making them rich, wise and powerful. Often, the best givers are physically poor, such as the widow. God does allow those who give to have sufficiency to continue giving. Paul affirmed this promise to those at Corinth who purposed in their heart and gave cheerfully: "And God is able to make all grace abound to you, that always having all sufficiency in everything, you may have an abundance for every good deed" (2 Corinthians 9:8).

We can notice a threefold motivation for giving. First, there is a desire to give when we become aware of the needs of other Christians. We are bound together in the body of Christ and have the same Holy Spirit dwelling in us. We are brothers and sisters; what affects one affects the other. The Christians in Macedonia exhibited this spirit when they heard of the needs of other Christians in Jerusalem. Paul said that they were anxious to help. They were "begging us with much entreaty for the favor of participation in the support of the saints" (2 Corinthians 8:4). There was a spirit of stewardship affirmed by Jesus Himself, "Freely you received, freely give" (Matthew 10:8). We must want to be good stewards of God's blessings.

Second, there is a desire to give because of compassion for those in need. Physical suffering, social rejection and spiritual lostness exist all around us. People need the help we can give.

The Pharisees criticized Jesus for reaching out to those who were the "left outs," the "passed over" and the "lost." Matthew, himself a tax collector, could identify with these people. He recorded this event which took place in his house:

> And when the Pharisees saw this, they said to His disciples, "Why is your Teacher eating with the tax-gatherers and sinners?" But when [Jesus] heard this, He said, "It is not those who are healthy who need a physician, but those who are sick. But go and learn what this means: 'I desire compassion, and not sacrifice' " (Matthew 9:11-13).

Jesus quoted from Hosea 6:6 to show that compassion had priority over sacrifice. This, the only Old Testament Scripture quoted twice by Jesus, shows both His own heart of compassion and a model for His disciples to follow.

The purpose of the contributions taken every first day of the week in Jesus' church should not be for self-indulgence, self-glorification and self-centered activities. The purpose should focus on the needy. Suffering bodies, broken hearts and lost souls abound. Meeting benevolent needs with compassion is one of the purposes of making a contribution. Paul spoke of this as a purpose of the contribution he was collecting: "For the ministry of this service is not only fully supplying the needs of the saints, but is also overflowing through many thanksgivings to God" (2 Corinthians 9:12). Our weekly contribution should begin in the heart of desire, take shape in the mind of planning and find fulfillment in the hand of doing.

Third, there is a desire to give because of the piety we learn in response to the grace of God. We stand in awe at the grace of God and the sacrifice of Jesus. This awesome humility is a primary motive for giving. Paul spoke of this in his instructions to the Corinthian Christians about giving:

But just as you abound in everything, in faith and utterance and knowledge and in all earnestness and in
the love we inspired in you, see that you abound in this
gracious work also. I am not speaking this as a command, but as proving through the earnestness of others the sincerity of your love also. For you know the
grace of our Lord Jesus Christ, that though He was rich,
yet for your sake He became poor, that you through
His poverty might become rich (2 Corinthians 8:7-9).

Three points from this text show the importance and the purpose of giving. First, learning to give is a part of Christian maturity. The Corinthian Christians were already abounding in faith,
utterances and knowledge; they needed to give the same attention to their giving. Second, their giving was a "proof" of their love.
Love by its very nature wants to give. Paul said that what we give
reflects our love for the Lord. Later he exhorted, "Therefore open-
ly before the churches show them the proof of your love and of
our reason for boasting about you" (2 Corinthians 8:24). Third,
their giving was a response to the grace of Jesus Christ, who was
rich but became poor for our benefit. That enabled us to become
rich. Paul called this "the grace of our Lord Jesus Christ."

OUTWARD EXPRESSION OF GIVING

Giving is always a response to a need. The church at Antioch
heard about a need in Judea and gave to help that need. Paul
reported to the churches of Macedonia and Achaia about the
needs of the poor saints at Jerusalem.

In preparation for collecting funds to help the poor saints at
Jerusalem, Paul provided Corinth a systematic plan for giving:

Now concerning the collection for the saints, as I directed the churches of Galatia, so do you also. On the
first day of every week let each one of you put aside
and save, as he may prosper, that no collections be
made when I come (1 Corinthians 16:1-2).

Notice four details in the text that serve as a model for raising
funds to support the work of the church. First, each one was to

participate in the giving. Second, the giving was to be done on the first day of the week, the day of assembly. Third, it was to be done "every" first day of the week. Fourth, what one gave was guided by prosperity.

MODEL FOR GIVING

Luke gave an account of the contribution the Antioch church sent to the Judeans, providing a snapshot of early church giving:

> And one of them named Agabus stood up and began to indicate by the Spirit that there would certainly be a great famine all over the world. And this took place in the reign of Claudius. And in the proportion that any of the disciples had means, each of them determined to send a contribution for the relief of the brethren living in Judea. And this they did, sending it in charge of Barnabas and Saul to the elders (Acts 11:28-30).

From this text we can gain five very important points about giving in the apostolic church. First came a need. Agabus, inspired by the Spirit, told of a famine that would hit "all the world." Especially affected by the famine would be the Christians in Judea. Second, there was total response from the church in Antioch. The text says, "Each one of them." The response was according to the means each person had. Third, the Christians wanted to give. The text says, "Each of them determined to send" – a thoughtful, willed response to the need. Fourth, they did what they determined to do. They didn't forget about it. They willed to do it. They planned to do it. Then they did it. Fifth, they sent it to the elders by the hands of Barnabas and Saul. Note how the Christians handled funds: via responsible people. Elders who knew the people's needs administered the distribution. No extra-congregational benevolent institutions were involved.

THE EVIL EYE

In Jesus' sermon on materialism, He used an analogy which many have misunderstood. It dealt with "good" and "evil" eyes.

Some versions call them "clear" and "bad" eyes. The context shows that Jesus was referring to how we look at life.

Moments earlier, Jesus had spoken of the folly of laying up treasures on earth. Moments later, He stressed that it is impossible to serve two masters – God and money. He was teaching about how people should use wealth in the best way. He discussed the foolishness of using wealth to hoard physical things, which wear out, rust out and are stolen by thieves. We best use wealth by activating it for spiritual values. These values do not wear out, rust out or get stolen. Jesus said, "Do not lay up for yourselves treasures upon earth, ... [b]ut lay up for yourselves treasures in heaven, ... for where your treasure is, there will your heart be also" (Matthew 6:19-21).

Our use of physical things influences both our reward in heaven and our outlook on life in the here and now. This was the meaning of Jesus' teachings about the "single" and "evil" eyes (KJV):

> The lamp of the body is the eye; if therefore your eye is clear, your whole body will be full of light. But if your eye is bad, your whole body will be full of darkness. If therefore the light that is in you is darkness, how great is that darkness! (Matthew 6:22-23).

The difficulty in understanding this passage is in identifying the meaning of the "clear" and "bad" eye. The word translated "clear" is *haplous* and is sometimes translated "single" (KJV, ASV), "good" (NIV) and "clear" (NASB). The word translated "bad" is *poneros* and is translated "evil" (KJV, ASV), and "bad" (NASB, NIV).

We can better understand the passage if we translate the words as "generous" and "stingy," terms used in translating *haplous* and *poneros* in the Septuagint (see Proverbs 22:9; 23:6). These translations better fit the context of Jesus' sermon on materialism. A paraphrase of the text might read something like this: "The quality of our life is determined by how we looks at things. If our heart is generous, we will have sunshine in our soul. If our heart is stingy, our whole life will be full of gloom and despair."

Paul quoted a saying of Jesus not found in the Gospels which affirms the blessings of generous giving: "It is more blessed to give than to receive" (Acts 20:35). Generous giving is "more blessed" because it preserves both our treasures in heaven and enriches the quality of our life on the earth.

SUGGESTIONS FOR WORSHIPING IN GIVING

1. When teaching on giving, focus more on the facts that it is worship and that it involves an awesome, humble submission to God rather than the dollars and cents needed to meet a budget.

2. When seeking to increase the weekly contribution, emphasize the attitude of generosity rather than duty in giving.

3. When seeking a special contribution to meet a pressing need, seek the participation of "every one."

4. Be sure to give reports on how earlier contributions have met needs.

5. Make available an accurate accounting of the funds collected and how they have been distributed.

6. Offer prayers of thanksgiving for our prosperity and help in our generosity.

SUMMARY

Giving is an act of worship. It is the humble submissive response of the inner man involving spirit, mind and heart to the awesome majesty of God. Giving is both a command from God and an apostolic example of the early church. It is an expression of fellowship in sharing one's blessings with those who have needs.

The New Testament provides a model for giving in the church. It is to be done by everyone according to individual prosperity and the willingness of each heart. It is to be done every first day of the week when Christians come together.

Wise is the giver who models giving after these passages:

> [L]ay up for yourselves treasures in heaven, where neither moth nor rust destroys, and where thieves do not break in or steal; for where your treasure is, there will your heart be also (Matthew 6:20-21).

It is more blessed to give than to receive (Acts 20:35).

And in the proportion that any of the disciples had means, each of them determined to send a contribution for the relief of the brethren living in Judea. And this they did (Acts 11:29-30).

Let each one do just as he has purposed in his heart; not grudgingly or under compulsion; for God loves a cheerful giver (2 Corinthians 9:7).

QUESTIONS

1. How can giving be classified as an act of worship?
2. Discuss the threefold inner motivation for giving.
3. Show four points 1 Corinthians 16:1-2 teaches on giving.
4. What Old Testament passage did Jesus quote twice?
5. Discuss how the giving of the church in Antioch is a model for the church today.
6. Explain the meaning of a "single eye" and an "evil eye" in Matthew 6:22-23.

CHAPTER ELEVEN

WORSHIP IN HEARING GOD'S WORD

2 Kings 22:1-23:25; Nehemiah 8:1-18; Jeremiah 36:23;
Luke 4:16-21; 2 Timothy 3:15-17; Hebrews 5:11-14; 12:18-29

Just as we worship by talking to God through prayer, we worship by listening to God through His Word. Through both, we commune with Deity. Both God and we act in the dynamics of prayer; both God and we act in the dynamics of "hearing the word of the Lord." In one, we are the awesome, humble, submissive speaker to Divinity. In the other, we are the awesome, humble, submissive listener to Divinity. The thought that God is listening to our praise and petitions in every prayer we speak is awesome. It is just as awesome to think that God is speaking His will in the words of the Scripture.

Worship in prayer expresses the yearnings of our hearts to God. Worship in hearing His Word is an act of receiving into our hearts the desires of God's heart. The hearer is not passive. We open our ears to hear, our mind to understand, and our heart to believe. In this process, worship takes place. The Bereans were commended because "they received the word with great eagerness" (Acts 17:11). The noble prayer asks, "Open our hearts and minds to receive Thy word." Nowhere in Scripture is hearing the word of the Lord identified as worship or an act of worship. We call it worship because it fits the definition and purposes of worship.

The Importance of Hearing God's Word

Only through hearing God's Word can we know His will, His Son Jesus and the Holy Spirit. The heavens declare His glory. The evidence of nature affirms His existence. Reason demands a first cause. The Scriptures, however, reveal His nature and His purpose for man. Everything else is human speculation. Jesus condemned the Pharisees for refusing to accept the testimony of the Scriptures: "You search the Scriptures, because you think that in them you have eternal life; and it is these that bear witness of Me" (John 5:39).

Only through hearing God's Word can we come to believe in Jesus. Paul affirmed that "faith comes from hearing, and hearing by the word of Christ" (Romans 10:17).

Only through hearing God's Word can we really know the will of God for our life. It is not enough to rely on the traditions of the past, the assimilations from the culture, a dynamic religious leader or theological religious speculations. All these are of human origin and are fallible. The only spiritual truth we can know comes from God in His word. Jesus said, "Thy word is truth" (John 17:17). Paul often appealed to Scripture to support His teachings by saying, "What saith the Scriptures?"

Only through hearing God's Word can we obtain Christian maturity. Readers of Hebrews were condemned because of their lack of growth. The key to their immaturity was their lack of knowing and doing the will of God:

> For though by this time you ought to be teachers, you
> have need again for someone to teach you the ele-
> mentary principles of the oracles of God, and you have
> come to need milk and not solid food. For everyone
> who partakes only of milk is not accustomed to the
> word of righteousness, for he is a babe. But solid food
> is for the mature (Hebrews 5:12-14).

The writer again affirmed the reason for their immaturity as being the neglect of the word of God:

> For this reason we must pay much closer attention to what we have heard, lest we drift away from it. ... [H]ow shall we escape if we neglect so great a salvation? After it was at the first spoken through the Lord, it was confirmed to us by those who heard (Hebrews 2:1, 3).

Only through hearing God's Word can we prepare for the final judgment. God has borne testimony that Jesus was the Christ, the Son of God by His miraculous birth, His inspired teachings, His miracles, and finally His resurrection. To reject Him and His teaching means condemnation. Jesus said, "He who rejects Me, and does not receive My sayings, has one who judges him; the word I spoke is what will judge him at the last day" (John 12:48). Hearing the Word of God becomes even more important when we realize that His Word is the basis of our final judgment.

THE AWESOME POWER OF GOD'S WORD

Try to imagine the awesome scene at Mount Sinai when God gave His law. The mountain itself was holy because of God's presence in fire, in darkness and gloom, in wind and in awesome sounds. God spoke directly to the people. They were so afraid that they did not want God to speak directly to them any longer. They wanted God to speak through Moses. The mountain was so holy that if any beast touched the mountain it was to be stoned. The writer of Hebrews recounted this scene:

> For you have not come to a mountain that may be touched and to a blazing fire, and to darkness and gloom and whirlwind, and to the blast of a trumpet and the sound of words which sound was such that those who heard begged that no further word should be spoken to them. For they could not bear the command, "If even a beast touches the mountain, it will be stoned." And so terrible was the sight, that Moses said, "I am full of fear and trembling" (Hebrews 12:18-21).

The giving of the law on Sinai was an awesome, terrifying experience. God spoke His word to Israel. By this word they were to be guided, and by this word they were to be judged. The Hebrew writer used this event as an analogy to describe a scenario even more terrifying:

> See to it that you do not refuse Him who is speaking. For if those did not escape when they refused him who warned them on earth, much less shall we escape who turn away from Him who warns from heaven. ... [L]et us show gratitude, by which we may offer to God an acceptable service with reverence and awe; for our God is a consuming fire (Hebrews 12:25, 28-29).

We must not take God's Word lightly. It is awesome and powerful. We notice the power of His Word when we read Mary's reaction to the announcement of Jesus' birth. She was a virgin and asked, "How could this be?" It appeared impossible. But God's word will come to pass even if we do not know the how, why or when. The American Standard translation gives the most literal translation of the angel's response in Luke 1:37: "For no word from God shall be void of power." If God says something, it is so. If God promises something, it will come to pass.

The word of God created the worlds. Whatever God said in creation was so. Even now, the universe is sustained by the power of the word of God. The Scripture says God made the world and "upholds all things by the word of His power" (Hebrews 1:3). If the sustaining power of the word were for an instant withheld, then the universe would disintegrate into the nothingness from which it was formed.

The word of God has revealed His will. The Scriptures are God's inspired Word. They were written by holy men who spoke from God as they were "moved by the Holy Spirit" (2 Peter 1:21). They are absolutely true and answer every spiritual question that we need to know. Paul said that they are "profitable for teaching, for reproof, for correction, for training in righteousness; that the man of God may be adequate, equipped for every good work" (2 Timothy 3:16-17).

The word of God spoken by Jesus performed miracles. He who made the world and ordained the laws that govern it could change these laws at His will and word. He could say, "Arise," and the lame would walk. He could say, "Open your eyes," and the blind could see. He could say, "Come forth" and the dead could live. He spoke God's word, and it was powerful.

The word of God convicts hearts. The multitude heard the apostles preach the word of God as "the Spirit was giving them utterance" on the Day of Pentecost (Acts 2:4). The result was that the hearers were convicted of having a part in the crucifixion of Jesus: "[T]hey were pierced to the heart, and said to Peter and the rest of the apostles, 'Brethren, what shall we do?' " (Acts 2:37) The preached word of God had the power of convicting people of sin. It did then, and it does now. The writer of Hebrews described the penetrating power of the word of God:

> For the word of God is living and active and sharper than any two-edged sword, and piercing as far as the division of soul and spirit, of both joints and marrow, and able to judge the thoughts and intentions of the heart (Hebrews 4:12).

We must hear the word of God if we wish to know His will and believe His claims. No wonder those who spoke it often admonished their hearers, "He who has ears, let him hear."

THE WORD OF GOD AND RESTORATION

Reading the Scriptures precedes restoration and renewal among God's people. It is the motivation and the framework of recalling those who have gone into apostasy back to the will of God.

During the reign of Manasseh and Amon, Judah had gone into apostasy. Manasseh taught the people to worship idols and all the host of heaven and made his son pass through the fire. Amon, his son, "did evil in the sight of the Lord, as Manasseh his father had done" (2 Kings 21:20). When Josiah became king at age 8, Judah had already departed from the word of God. But Josiah was a good king who "did right in the sight of the Lord" (22:2).

In the 18th year of his reign, while repairing the temple, Hilkiah the high priest found the book of the law. It had no doubt been neglected, rejected and lost. Its reading brought about a restoration in Judah. This restoration came about because the book of the law was read, believed and obeyed. The story is told in 2 Kings:

> Then Hilkiah the high priest said to Shaphan the scribe, "I have found the book of the law in the house of the Lord." And Hilkiah gave the book to Shaphan who read it. ... And Shaphan read it in the presence of the king. And it came about when the king heard the words of the book of the law, that he tore his clothes. Then the king commanded Hilkiah, the priest ... saying, "Go, inquire of the Lord for me ... for great is the wrath of the Lord that burns against us, because our fathers have not listened to the words of this book, to do according to all that is written concerning us" (2 Kings 22:8, 10-13).

The book of the law had been found. Both a priest and a scribe had been instrumental in bringing it to the attention of the king. The king knew the seriousness of the situation and sought to know what the Lord wanted him to do. The king went up to the house of the Lord and read the book of the law to the people. This act resulted in a covenant between God, the king and the people:

> [H]e read in their hearing all the words of the book of the covenant which was found in the house of the Lord. And the king stood by the pillar and made a covenant before the Lord, to walk after the Lord, and to keep His commandments and His testimonies and His statutes with all his heart and all his soul (2 Kings 23:2-3).

Josiah kept the covenant he made and purged the land of all the different forms of idolatry. He began to observe all that Israel had neglected during its apostasy. The Passover feast which had been neglected since the days of the judges was restored. The reading of the word of God brought about restoration. Restoration meant both the removal of all that God had not authorized as well as the practice of all that God had authorized. It was said of Josiah,

> And before him there was no king like him who turned
> to the Lord with all his heart and with all his soul and
> with all his might, according to all the law of Moses;
> nor did any like him arise after him (2 Kings 23:25).

Observe the great contrast between Josiah and his ancestor, Solomon. Solomon had been given wisdom from God greater than all the wise men of the East and all of the wisdom of Egypt, yet he took foreign wives contrary to the commandments of God. These wives turned his heart away from God: "For it came about when Solomon was old, his wives turned his heart away after other gods; and his heart was not wholly devoted to the Lord his God, as the heart of David his father had been" (1 Kings 11:4). Solomon built high places to these false gods which remained until the days of Josiah's restoration.

> And the high places which were before Jerusalem,
> which were on the right of the mount of destruction
> which Solomon the king of Israel had built for Ashtoreth
> the abomination of the Sidonians, and for Chemosh the
> abomination of Moab, and for Milcom the abomination
> of the sons of Ammon, the king defiled (2 Kings 23:13).

Solomon, though having great wisdom, led Israel away from God because he ignored the word of God. Josiah, though only 26, led Israel back to God because he obeyed the book of the law.

Another great restoration came about in Israel because of the reading of the word of God. This happened during the return of the Jews from Babylonian captivity. Nehemiah had influenced King Artaxerxes to allow some of the Jews who had been taken into Babylonian captivity to return and rebuild Jerusalem. Many returned. They found that the temple had been destroyed, the wall of the city had fallen down and the city lay in ruins.

God called some men to bring about a restoration. Nehemiah led in restoring the wall. Zerubbabel led in restoring the temple. Ezra led in restoring the faith and religious teachings given by God to Moses. The religious restoration formed the basis for, and gave purpose to, the other restorations.

The reading of the book of the law of Moses enabled the restoration to take place. The Scriptures tell the story:

> Then Ezra the priest brought the law before the assembly of men, women, and all who could listen with understanding. ... [A]nd all the people were attentive to the book of the law. ... Ezra opened the book in the sight of all the people for he was standing above all the people; and when he opened it, all the people stood up. ... [A]nd the Levites, explained the law to the people. ... And they read from the book, from the law of God, translating to give the sense so that they understood the reading (Nehemiah 8:2-3, 5, 7-8).

The reading, the understanding and the believing of the book of the law of Moses led to a great restoration. The people made a public confession of sins. They observed the Feast of Tabernacles, neglected for many years. They excluded foreigners from the temple. They put away foreign wives. They sought to follow the book of the law given by Moses and to restore the true faith and practice of serving only Jehovah God.

The practice of a public reading of Scripture has a long history. In the cases of Josiah the king and Ezra the scribe, it brought about the restoration of the true faith of Israel. Jesus publicly read the Scriptures in the synagogue:

> And He came to Nazareth, where He had been brought up; and as was His custom, He entered the synagogue on the Sabbath, and stood up to read. And the book of the prophet Isaiah was handed to Him. And He opened the book, and found the place where it was written, "The Spirit of the Lord is upon Me ..." And He closed the book, and gave it back to the attendant and sat down (Luke 4:16-18, 20).

One of the things Paul told the young evangelist Timothy to prescribe and teach dealt with the public reading of Scriptures: "Until I come, give attention to the public reading of Scripture, to exhortation and teaching" (1 Timothy 4:13). The Word of God is holy, true and powerful. It reveals the will of God and produces faith in those who hear it with an open heart. It corrects religious errors and convicts hearts of sin. It guides restoration and is the substance of hope. Its reading can be worship because through it God speaks to us and we respond in awesome, humble submission.

THE SEED IS THE WORD OF GOD

The parable of the sower focuses on hearing the Word of God. After telling the story, Jesus said, "He who has ears, let him hear."

He interpreted the parable for His disciples. The sown seed is the word of God. The hearer who does not receive the word is like the hard soil beside the road. The hearer who at first receives it but later falls away is like rocky soil. The hearer who receives the word but then lets materialism crowd it out of his life is like the soil with thorns. The good soil refers to those who gladly receive the word of God and obey it: "And the one on whom seed was sown on the good soil, this is the man who hears the word and understands it; who indeed bears fruit" (Matthew 13:23). Worship in hearing the word of God involves not only God's speaking His word but also our receiving the word in an awesome, humble and submissive way.

The Bible was the first book to be printed. More Bibles are circulated in the world than any other book. Ignorance of the will of God is inexcusable in most of the world.

The Bible is read and revered in most Protestant and Catholic religions. Its stories are told to the children. It is often read before the people. It is considered holy. Its message, however, is often perverted or ignored. As with the Jews before the time of Josiah, the book of the will of God is neglected and rejected rather than respected.

Apostasy from the will of God begins not because the word of God is unknown but because it is unheeded. The writer of Hebrews identified this as the cause of Israel's apostasy in the wilderness. He then exhorted them to be hearers who obey:

> For indeed we have had good news preached to us, just as they also; but the word they heard did not profit them, because it was not united by faith in those who

heard. ... "Today if you hear His voice, do not hard-
en your hearts" (Hebrews 4:2, 7).

SUGGESTIONS FOR WORSHIP
IN HEARING THE WORD OF GOD

1. Devote time to the reading of Scriptures when the church
assembles. Sometimes the Scriptures can be read without com-
ments. Sometimes it is necessary to give the context and the
meaning of difficult words and phrases.

2. The Scripture reading should reflect the needs of the congregation or complement the focus of the other acts of worship.

3. The Scriptures should be read by one who reads well and
prepares for public reading by learning difficult words.

4. The attitude of the one reading Scriptures is that of awe, humility and submission. It is no time to get too dramatic or to speak
with a non-feeling mumble.

5. Public reading of Scripture should not become a cold ritual without meaning or purpose.

6. The congregation needs to show reverence for the word of
God. Those who heard Ezra reading sometimes stood and sometimes said, "Amen."

QUESTIONS

1. Discuss how speaking and hearing the Scriptures can be regarded as worship.
2. How is the power of the word of God shown in the following:
    • Creation   • Revelation
    • Miracles   • Conversion
3. Explain how the neglect of the Word of God brings apostasy
and the reading of the Word of God brings restoration.
4. What examples exist for reading the Scriptures in the assembly of the church?
5. In what way would the daily Bible reading of members of the
congregation help the church to grow and mature?
6. What does the parable of the sower teach about "receiving the
Word of God"?

BROTHERHOOD TENSIONS

Section 3 contains two chapters that bring into focus existing tensions among churches of Christ and identify their causes. Chapter 12 identifies some of these tensions and explains how they have evolved from the way the Scriptures are interpreted. Also discussed is the reactionary spirit among those who are on both the legalistic and the experiential extremes.

Chapter 13 reviews the basic scriptural criteria for determining acceptable and unacceptable worship to God. We can gauge current worship practices by the Scriptures to determine if they are apostolic traditions or human traditions.

A list of current issues is given at the end of Chapter 13. It is provided to clarify the real principles involved and stimulate class discussion. It is hoped that such discussion will do four things: First, it will bring hidden fears, motives and presuppositions out into the open and let them be examined in light of the Scriptures. Second, it will lead to better understanding of other points of view. Third, it will cause examination and evaluation of individual worship practices and stimulate personal spiritual growth. Fourth, it will identify those acts and attitudes which must be rejected as false worship.

CHAPTER TWELVE

THE STATE OF CHURCHES OF CHRIST

Acts 20:28-31; 2 Thessalonians 2:15; 3:7;
1 Timothy 4:2; 2 Timothy 4:1-4; Jude 3-16

Some of today's most talked-about tensions in the churches of Christ center upon worship by the assembled church. This is probably because worship in the "worship assembly" involves the total church with all of its diversities yet at the same time reflects the spiritual fellowship which ties these diversities together. Anything threatening this fellowship affects the life and even the existence of a local congregation.

A similar situation existed in the church in the first century and at the turn of the 20th century. Then, as now, existed cultural diversities, geographical separations, generational gaps, as well as different economic levels, social strata, educational attainments, ethnic backgrounds and philosophical outlooks. This was fine as long as these differences did not infringe upon the authority of Christ or the conscience of other Christians.

In 1889 controversies led to a division. Leaders of the church were discussing instrumental music, missionary societies, leadership roles for women and the authority of the Scriptures. In the 1906 United States census, the division between churches of Christ and the Disciples was formally recognized by the government. The Disciples later divided, creating the Independent Christian Church.

This division in the American Restoration Movement did not come about because of differences in theological opinions or geographical and social factors or even because of the civil war. The division came over doctrine.

Leaders in the Disciples Church and the Independent Christian Church held that the silence of the Scriptures was permissive. Leaders in churches of Christ held that the silence of the Scriptures was prohibitive. This view of the Scriptures on the part of the Disciples and the Independent Christian Church resulted in the unscriptural innovations of performance worship with instrumental music and choirs, missionary and aid societies which usurped the autonomy of local congregations and the loss of doctrinal distinctiveness from Protestant denominations.

Churches split, families divided and friends were estranged because of these issues. Not only were these innovations without scriptural authority; they also violated the conscience of those who opposed them. You can have a difference of opinion and still maintain fellowship. Differences in opinions should not affect the fellowship or the shared worship in the Christian assemblies. Differences in faith do.

Opinions are a matter of judgment, while faith is a matter of conviction. Opposition to performance worship, women worship leaders and open fellowship with denominational groups were matters of conviction. Those who opposed these innovations could not in good conscience be a part of what was introduced without scriptural authority.

Many of the same issues face the churches of Christ today. Many of the same cultural influences in our time were present a century ago. They are having the same effect on some in the church as they did on the people who led in the apostasy a century ago. The warning Paul gave to the elders at Ephesus fits our current struggles:

> Be on guard for yourselves and for all the flock, among which the Holy Spirit has made you overseers, to shepherd the church of God which He purchased with His own blood. I know that after my departure savage wolves will come in among you, not sparing the flock; and from among your own selves men will arise, speaking perverse things, to draw away disciples after them. Therefore be on the alert (Acts 20:28-31).

Unless there is a change of heart in the leaders of this new apostasy, many churches of Christ will lose their distinctiveness and hence their reason to exist. The result will be that institutions supported by members of the church of Christ will be compromised and innumerable souls will be lost.

FACTORS CREATING TENSION

Several factors being discussed in the contemporary tensions need clarification. Some are straw men, issues created to find an opponent that can be easily defeated. Some are real; we need to address them and make the necessary changes.

The tensions are not merely between the traditional and contemporary. As already noted, this is a straw man. Something is not necessarily bad if it is old or necessarily good if it is contemporary. Neither is something good just because it is old. If traditions are apostolic, they are binding; if they are human, they are not to be bound. If a contemporary practice finds justification in Scripture, it is binding; if it does not, it must not be imposed upon others in the church.

Much of what is spoken and written about worship is reactionary. It has always been easy to find isolated examples of cold, legalistic, traditional and empty worship practices. These kinds of practices are not correct; nor are they the norm. Those who criticize the church as being legalistic and cold often are reflecting more about their own impoverished spiritual background than about the real church.

The same is true about those who cry, "Wolf! Wolf!" and give examples of a few churches in some places who have practiced unscriptural worship. Some of these examples are valid and need to be opposed, but false rumors and uncritical exaggerations abound.

Those who consider themselves as being on the cutting edge of change continue to see how far they can move to the "liberal" extreme without losing their influence among the churches. They want to retain their traditional identity in churches of Christ and at the same time destroy the biblical identity which makes her more congruent with God's Word and as a result more distinctive in the religious community.

Some of those who like to call themselves "conservative" think of themselves as saviors of the church. They see wrong and want to right it. They see error and want to correct it. They see the coming apostasy and want to refute it. This is fine, but such a mission can and sometimes does become an obsession. They look for things to oppose and become "watchdogs" of the brotherhood. They hear or read of something amiss in some far-off place, and without questioning its source they disparage it as if it were true. Obsessed by the threat of apostasy, they lose sight of the "good news" of the gospel message or the many positive and glorious things happening in the brotherhood.

The extremes of the far right and the extremes of the far left are not the norm, and I refuse to be identified with either one. A motto to live by in our current struggles is, "Striving to be biblical in teaching, conservative in practice and liberal in love."

Some would like to make these issues between the old and the young. It is true that those who become absorbed with the culture of either the past or the present do have a different outlook on life. The teachings of our Lord, however, are non-generational. I refuse to be pegged as either "builder" or "boomer." When I became a Christian, I erased such generational barriers. "That's the way we've always done it" is not a sufficient reason to oppose change. "That's the way everyone else is doing it" is not a sufficient reason to advocate change. "What does the Bible say?" is reason enough. "Will it edify my brother?" is a major consideration.

Identifying ourselves with the human traditions of the church in the past will make the church of Christ no more than the

"church of the past culture." Identifying ourselves with the contemporary culture will make the church of Christ no more than
the "church of the times." To be the church of Christ means that
we identify ourselves with the church's Founder, whose teachings guide her and will someday judge her.

Church growth is an excuse some give for adding unscriptural innovations to the worship of the church. There is a whole
body of literature promoting church growth by secular means.
It is designed to meet the "felt needs" of people. It can be effec-
tive for temporarily increasing membership and filling the pews.

Tailoring worship to meet "felt needs" has its weaknesses,
though. These perceived needs of people are not necessarily the
real spiritual needs of the soul. Idolatry seeks to fill the felt needs
of many. The secular attraction often suggested in church growth
literature deals with social involvement, entertainment attractions
and experiential stimulation. None of these have valid spiritual
content. People attracted to such things will be attracted to another group as soon as it offers something they like better.

Real church growth comes from the Gospel being taught to
warn people of sin and its consequences. This message convicts
the lost and motivates them to repent and obey in baptism. They
become loyal to Christ. They commit to following His will to meet
the real spiritual needs of the soul.

This is not to say that there is nothing to learn from church
growth literature. It often gives helpful guidance in the skills of
human relations, organization and communication. We should
reject, however, the secular emphases of its methods. Consider
Jesus' focus: He ministered to people's physical and emotional
needs, but He then dealt with their spiritual problems.

Similarly, Christ's church devotes itself to the welfare of the total person. Benevolent outreach touches the physical needs, and
Christian fellowship deals with human relationships. The gospel
message, however, deals with the spiritual part of a person. This
is what is central.

Despite loosening the doctrinal restrictions of the Scriptures
to gain "members," welcoming into fellowship those who are "be-

lievers only" to fill the pews; despite giving the masses what they want in religious performances; and despite changing the great commission into social, recreational and counseling missions, non-distinctive denominations are not growing. Flavil Yeakley notes in his book *Separating Fact from Fiction* that the Disciples of Christ, for example, are the fastest declining religious institution in the United States.

Here is a consistent statistic of many congregations I have seen that seek to cater to the culture: they are not baptizing many people. Non-distinctive churches of Christ are destined to follow their theological predecessors, the Disciples of Christ.

It is folly to try to build a church of the Lord as you would build a "church of the culture." Jesus did not assimilate with the culture; He confronted it.

SCRIPTURE INTERPRETATION

Perhaps the most serious underlying tension among churches of Christ is that some of the thought leaders have a low view of the Scriptures.

On the one hand, some have a low view of the Scriptures by regarding them as no more than a collection of proof texts to be used in debate. They have little regard for the immediate, secondary or total context of Scripture. This view creates the non-class party, the one-cup party, the divorce-for-any-cause party and the charismatic party.

On the other hand, some have a low view of the Scriptures by regarding them as writing which must be interpreted experientially, culturally and relatively. An experiential interpretation places inspiration in the reader. The text is merely the words of men in an ancient culture. It becomes the word of God as it is experientially interpreted. It means what "you feel" it says. This existential understanding is accepted no matter how different it might be from the language, context and grammar of the text. According to this view, one's interpretation does not need to be consistent with another person's interpretation or even one's own interpretation at a different time. Using this kind of interpretation, a text means what you want it to mean at any time and any place.

A cultural interpretation is often combined with the experiential interpretation. This presupposes that the original text was written in and for an ancient culture and is irrelevant to our present situation. Ancient people possessed an entirely different world view, were influenced by different customs and lived in a primitive culture. Text meant one thing to them, but it can mean something entirely different to us. Using this kind of interpretation, a text means what you want it to mean.

Many use this kind of interpretation to modify what Paul taught about the role of women in the church. He said, "Let your women keep silent in the churches." Contrary to what some teach, this was not a cultural thing. The cultural situation at Corinth or a supposed gender bias of Paul had nothing to do with this teaching. Paul affirmed the source of his teachings very clearly: "If anyone thinks he is a prophet or spiritual, let him recognize that the things which I write to you are the Lord's commandment" (1 Corinthians 14:37).

A relative interpretation is usually combined with the experiential and cultural interpretations, which by their nature are relative. One is relative because it rests on the changing and contradictory experiences of people; the other is relative because it rests upon the changing cultures of people. These methods of interpretation fit many of the presuppositions of our contemporary culture, which regards all truth as relative. This means that you can have "your truth" and I can have "my truth." Neither is absolute; truth is only what one perceives it to be. Using any one of these methods of interpretation, a text means what you want it to mean at any time and any place. But this is what Jesus said about truth being absolute and knowable. He taught, "Thy word is truth" and "you shall know the truth" (John 17:17; 8:32).

PERMISSIVE SILENCE

Another kind of interpretation already mentioned as being a primary cause of the division in the American Restoration

Movement is permissive silence . That is, "If the Scriptures do not specifically condemn something, we may practice it." This interpretation led not only to instrumental music in the Disciples Church but also to the burning of candles, the burning of incense, holy water and a multitude of other innovations in the Roman Catholic Church.

The opposite of permissive silence is prohibitive silence. That is, "We must reject any innovation in the worship or work of the church that is not directly authorized or implied by Scripture."

Jesus understood that the Scriptures were to be interpreted by prohibitive silence. In His temptation, the devil showed Him all of the kingdoms of the world and said, "All these things will I give You, if You fall down and worship me" (Matthew 4:9).

The answer Jesus gave showed that He used prohibitive silence in His interpretation of the Scriptures. He quoted Deuteronomy 6:13. The Hebrew text reads, "You shall fear the Lord your God; and you shall worship Him." Moses understood that by telling Israel who they were to worship excluded all of the gods of the Egyptians, Moabites, Canaanites and any other so-called gods. Jesus did, too. He knew that it excluded the devil. The text in Matthew added a word not found in the Hebrew text of Deuteronomy 6: "only." That confirmed that He understood the silence of the Scriptures to be prohibitive. His disciples should have the same lofty view of the Scriptures.

A SPIRIT OF DIVISIVENESS

One of the most serious points of tension in the brotherhood is the spirit of divisiveness. We find it in the networks of preachers, conclaves of congregations, attendees at certain lectureships and subscribers to certain papers. People form religious cliques which exclude anyone who does not follow the party line. Leaders arise as "keepers of orthodoxy" within the group, whose identity is found not so much in what it believes and teaches so much as what it opposes and slanders.

One group wants to change the brotherhood back to the way it was in the 1950s – whatever that was.

Another group wants to change the brotherhood to conform to the present culture – whatever that is.

Hopefully, most people do not want to be a part of the bickering; they merely want to return to simple New Testament Christianity, follow the teachings of the Lord and love the brotherhood.

Leaders of all groups play politics: How can we gain control of and change this school, this paper or this congregation? Take two steps forward toward change and then one step backward to appease the opposition. Take your time. Get people in key positions and have them ready for a "takeover." Talk "brotherly love" but practice slander. Pit one generation against another, the rich against the poor and the elite against the common people. Divide and conquer.

The battle lines are drawn. The problem is that most Christians in most congregations do not want war. They want peace. They pray for harmony. As long as a majority of those who are members of the church of Christ refuse to be sectarian and continue to reject the party spirit, the war can be avoided. This will mean paying attention to these exhortations:

1. Be scriptural! The brotherhood traditions of the past and the allurement of the present culture must not woo us from the ideal of "speaking where the Bible speaks and being silent where the Bible is silent."

2. Be honest! If you believe something to be true, do not be ashamed to declare it. If you doubt something to be true, do not be afraid to say so. Too long has a scandal of silence allowed error to go unchallenged and truth to be hidden.

3. Be loving! We are to do more than just love those who love us; we must love our enemies and those who persecute us and speak evil of us. That is what God does, and that is what His children need to do.

4. Be bold! Christians grow confident not because of who we are, but whose we are. We grow confident because of the need for our message and its truthfulness. We grow confident because we have the help of God. We grow confident because of what God has done in our own life.

5. Be an exhorter! Even when things go bad, we can still find something good. Exhorters look for the good, the beautiful and the true. Exhorters make others feel better about themselves and their surroundings.

6. Do not become involved in parties! They destroy the church and pervert the minds of those who espouse them. In every generation there are those who are sloughed off from the body of Christ because they have developed a party spirit. The same will be true in this generation. Even the Apostle John had to recognize that "[t]hey went out from us, but they were not really of us" (1 John 2:19).

Tensions exist in churches of Christ. They always have and always will. We should not ignore them. We should challenge them with understanding and truth. This chapter seeks to get at the real causes of these tensions and provide a forum for their discussion. Most tensions involve the worship of the church, but an underlying cause is to be found in different views of the Scriptures.

QUESTIONS

1. Name some of the similarities between the present state of churches of Christ and the divisive forces at work in the American Restoration Movement near the close of the 19th century.
2. What is the difference between opinion and faith? Give Biblical examples and contemporary examples.
3. Show ways the extreme "liberals" and extreme "conservatives" react to one another.
4. What is the difference between "prohibitive silence" and "permissive silence" in understanding Scriptures? Give examples.
5. What do word meanings, context and grammar have to do with interpreting Scriptures? Give an example of an experiential interpretation of Scriptures.
6. Give six suggestions that can help nullify the party spirit in a congregation.

CHAPTER THIRTEEN

TENSION IN WORSHIP PRACTICES

Leviticus 10:1-2; Deuteronomy 17:14;
Matthew 15:8-9; Acts 14:15; Romans 1:21-23; 14:13;
1 Corinthians 6:14-17; 8:11-12; 14:1-40; 15:33;
Colossians 3:16; 2 Timothy 3:7; Revelation 2:20

This chapter will deal with innovative worship practices within churches of Christ. First, it will distinguish between "expedients and innovations." Next, it will identify some of the points of tension caused by innovative worship practices. Third, it will propose criteria for judging these issues in light of the Scriptures and in brotherly love.

EXPEDIENTS

A number of traditional practices surrounding worship fall into a category that can be called "expedients." They consist of things for which there is no scriptural authority. They merely carry out a worship practice authorized in Scripture.

An expedient is an option that expedites a commanded worship practice. It neither adds to nor takes away from what is being done. Using a song book, selecting a number and even having a song leader are all expedients for worshiping in song. Nothing is added to or taken away from worshiping in song. The expedients assist with orderliness and edification.

An example of an expedient, as previously mentioned, is the white cloth which in times past was used to cover the grape juice and the unleavened bread on the communion table. For that matter, the communion table itself is an expedient. So is a gospel meeting. Even the invitation song at the close of the sermon, a practical, time-honored custom, is nothing more than an aid to the scriptural exhortation of admonishing each other in song (Colossians 3:16).

A human innovation is something added to worship that is not divinely authorized. It can be praying to God through a graven image. It can be lighting candles and burning incense as devotion to God. It can be singing praises to God with instrumental music. An innovation is anything unauthorized that is added to God-ordained worship acts.

Let's ask four questions when considering a potential expedient.

First, does it expedite the worship practice or does it add to the worship practice? Is it really what it claims to be, or is it an addition to a divinely authorized practice? The strange fire offered by Nadab and Abihu was not an expedient. It was an addition which God "had not commanded them" (Leviticus 10:1).

Second, is it decent and orderly? Everybody talking at the same time, speaking in a foreign language without an interpreter and allowing women to speak in the assembly were all disorderly conduct in the church at Corinth (1 Corinthians 14:26-40). These activities were not an expedient to a worship practice. They brought confusion. The same is true of similar conduct two millennia later.

Third, is it edifying to other participants in worship? Worship in community must be understandable. It must involve both the spirit and the understanding (1 Corinthians 14:15-16). Whatever hinders the understanding of a worship practice is not an expedient. It is foolishness.

Fourth, does it offend a brother or sister? If the conscience of someone is offended by some expedient unnecessary in fulfilling a worship practice, it should not be forced upon that person. This offensive thing involves more than mere personal preference. It involves a change driven by preference which puts Christians in a position of doing something they believe to be wrong. Brotherly love demands the omission or rejection of the innovation. Paul addresses such a situation at Corinth: "For through your knowledge he who is weak is ruined, the brother for whose sake Christ died. And thus, by sinning against the brethren and wounding their conscience when it is weak, you sin against Christ" (1 Corinthians 8:11-12).

We have a lot of liberty involved in the use of expedients. We may sing an invitation song after the closing prayer, at the beginning of the assembly or not at all. We may sing in unison, in four-part harmony or chant. We may pour the grape juice – or wine – into one cup or many cups. Teachers and preachers can read from the King James Version or other translations.

Human Innovations

Human innovations in worship practices should cause tension because they have no scriptural authority and are not an expedient way of fulfilling an authorized worship practice. They are wrong and should be opposed and rejected.

Human innovations consist of such practices as adding roasted lamb to the unleavened bread and grape juice used in the Lord's supper or burning incense as a part of worshiping in prayer. Other innovations would be using instrumental music as a part of worshiping in song, practicing ecstatic utterances called glossolalia in addition to teaching the Word of God and having raffles and bake sales to supplement the worship of giving to the Lord.

Nadab and Abihu were consumed with fire from the Lord because of the innovation of "strange fire" in their worship (Leviticus 10:1-2). Many of Israel's kings were condemned because of the innovation of idols into Israel's worship practices. Jesus condemned the Pharisees who added human innovations to their worship practices, quoting from Isaiah 29:13: "This people honors Me with their lips, but their heart is far away from Me. But in vain do they worship Me, teaching as doctrines the precepts of men" (Matthew 15:8-9).

The desire for human innovations to worship practices stems from different motivations. Some people are ignorant of the Scriptures and are willing to try any new thing, particularly if they are immature or flawed in their understanding of worship. They seem to think something new and different might make their worship practices become more meaningful. But a change of practice cannot be substituted for a change of heart. Paul taught that neglect of true worship to the real God led to the worship of idols:

> For even though they knew God, they did not honor Him as God, or give thanks; ... and their foolish heart was darkened. Professing to be wise, they became fools, and exchanged the glory of the incorruptible God for an image in the form of corruptible man and of birds and four-footed animals and crawling creatures (Romans 1:21-23).

Not only is "an empty mind the devil's workshop," but also "an empty heart is the devil's sanctuary." Neglect of true worship is probably the chief cause of the innovations in false worship.

Some people are rebellious, set on changing things for the sake of change. Like those Paul refuted at Ephesus, they are "always learning and never able to come to the knowledge of the truth" (2 Timothy 3:7). They subscribe to the thinking that "the old is bad and the new is good" without thinking about it critically. They do not want an inherited faith from the past; they want a "faith of their own." But in seeking a "faith of their own," they not only reject the human traditions of the past, but they also embrace the human traditions of the present. They become free from the shackles of past cultures only to bind themselves with the chains of the contemporary culture. They have not been liberated; they have only changed masters.

Some people just want to be like others around them. Being different or distinct is out of their comfort zone. They, like Israel, want to be "like all the nations who are around" (Deuteronomy 17:14). They have not learned the truthfulness of Paul's warning to the Corinthians: "Do not be deceived: 'Bad company corrupts good morals'" (1 Corinthians 15:33). God wanted Israel to be a distinct and holy nation when it entered Canaan. He warned His children not to assimilate with the pagans who lived in the land: "You shall make no covenant with them and show no favor to them. Furthermore, you shall not intermarry with them; ... For they will turn your sons away from following Me to serve other gods" (Deuteronomy 7:2-4).

The Corinthians had a problem with the assimilation of pagan religious practices. They were surrounded by idol worshipers who practiced all kinds of worship ceremonies and rituals in the name of false gods. Paul warned them:

> Do not be bound together with unbelievers; for what partnership have righteousness and lawlessness, or what fellowship has light with darkness? Or what harmony has Christ with Belial, or what has a believer in common with an unbeliever? Or what agreement has the temple of God with idols? ... "Therefore, come out from their midst and be separate," says the Lord. "And do no touch what is unclean" (2 Corinthians 6:14-17).

Some people are passive. They do not have enough conviction to care. They take the course of least resistance. They are afraid to object to false teachings lest they offend someone. They want an easy, comfortable religion in which they can believe anything, tolerate everybody and worship any way. That which is so liberal and loose means nothing. Whoever believes that one faith is as good as another cannot hold to absolute truth; absolute truth presupposes that something is false. Whoever tolerates everybody's religion also gives approval to false faiths. This kind of toleration is, in reality, an act of non-love. In the name of tolerance, those in sin and error are lost eternally.

Whoever practices or gives sanction to erroneous worship falls under the judgment of God. Jesus condemned the church at Thyatira for tolerating immoral conduct and false worship:

> I have this against you, that you tolerate the woman
> Jezebel, who calls herself a prophetess, and she teach-
> es and leads My bond-servants astray so that they com-
> mit acts of immorality and eat things sacrificed to idols
> (Revelation 2:20).

Jezebel was condemned, but a greater condemnation rested upon the church that tolerated her false teachings.

The church today needs Christians with the boldness of Barnabas and Paul, who stood in the midst of pagan idolatry at Lystra and confronted the people for their false worship to false gods. The people considered Paul and Barnabas to be incarnate gods, but the two refused to receive worship. Paul and Barnabas said,

> Men, why are you doing these things? We are also men
> of the same nature as you, and preach the gospel to
> you in order that you should turn from these vain
> things to a living God, who made the heaven and the
> earth and the sea, and all that is in them (Acts 14:15).

ISSUES OF TENSION

No one can doubt that tensions of worship practices exist among churches of Christ today. Some preachers have gone into human denominations because of their desire for worship innovations. Some churches have split. Some churches are in the process of splitting by having separate assemblies, calling each one "a different style of worship." Some congregations have tensions which have arisen between generational groups. Many preachers, elders, deacons and members are in confusion trying to listen to everybody and yet are doing nothing.

Rather than writing a argumentative book condemning wrongs, I want to affirm the definition and nature of worship, identify its sources, forms and purposes and also distinguish the difference between expedients and innovations. By doing this, we can arrive at the basic principles that can determine what is and what is not acceptable worship to God.

The tensions that need to be discussed in many congregations include the following:

1. Is worship an everyday lifestyle or specific acts? What is the definition of worship? How is an analogy to be understood?

2. Is singing exclusively congregational, or can groups and individuals sing for the edification of others? Does being in or out of the assembled church have bearing on the answer? How about funerals and weddings?

3. Are clapping and hand raising ever acceptable in praying and singing? Are kneeling and the head bowing/eye-closing practices acceptable? Do the cultural meanings of a practice and the individual's purpose for doing it have bearing on the answer?

4. Can the Lord's Supper be observed other than with the assembled church on the first day of the week? Can the unleavened bread and grape juice be changed or added to?

5. Can women be worship leaders in the assembled church? Can they be worship leaders in a non-public class or a devotional of mixed genders?

6. Can instrumental music be used with worship in song in the assembled church? Can it be used with worship in song in a private setting?

7. Can a Christian participate in unscriptural worship? Can a Christian be a part of a fellowship that practices unscriptural worship?

8. Can a Christian publicly read from any translation of the Scriptures other than the King James Version and the American Standard Versions and their revisions?

9. Is a song leader scriptural or an expedient? Is an invitation song scriptural or an expedient? Is saying "amen" scriptural or an expedient? Is giving in the contribution on the first day of the week scriptural or an expedient?

10. Can a Christian participate in singing songs not in the regular songbook? Songs that are sung in unison? Songs that are sung antiphonally? Songs that are chants?

11. Can a congregation have two different assemblies on Sunday because of space limitations and occupational constraints? Can they have two different assemblies because of generational differences, "worship style" prejudice or cultural isolation?

CRITERIA FOR JUDGING

The key factor in these discussions is does it please God? Worshiping God involves the inner devotion of worshipers as we approach God. Our being is filled with awe of His majesty; our spirit has an attitude of humble submission. We respond to Divinity with external acts of devotion prescribed by God and coming from our total being. We commune spiritually with the holiness of the eternal spiritual God. Four criteria need to govern how we worship.

First, worship practices must have divine authorization. They must not be left to our discretion. What most of the people want makes no difference. What is popular in the culture makes no difference. What thought leaders in the church, whether past or present, have said makes no difference. The what, why, when and how of worship must come from divine authority.

Second, worship must come from the right source. It must not be "word-only" worship. It must not be empty, meaningless rituals handed down from the past. It must not be merely experientially responding to "performance worship." Worship must involve not only the right external forms but also the total internal being. Worship involves our spirit, the part of us that wills and loves. No one can worship who does not will to. Worship involves our mind, our rational being. We must understand and mean what we are saying and doing for worship to take place. Worship involves our heart, our emotional being. When we worship, we must involve not only our will and understanding, but also our feelings. Our heart overflows with praise and yearns for God's favor.

Third, worship must have valid purposes. It is more than traditional ritualistic duty. It is not an attempt to manipulate God or to win the favor of others. It involves three basic purposes. The first purpose is to express the praise and devotion arising from inside. The surge of spiritual feelings is sometimes so strong that we must cry out in praise and petitions.

The second purpose is to magnify and glorify God. Aware of His presence and His gracious care for us, we join the angels in the throne room of heaven in singing, "Worthy Art Thou."

The third purpose comes from worship in community. We are concerned not only with our inner selves and the God-sanctioned forms and but also with our fellow worshipers. Worship must be understood for hearers to be edified. It must be done in a decent and orderly way.

Fourth, we should not practice worship expedients that would offend a weak brother or sister. Paul's admonition to the church at Rome is still relevant today: "Therefore let us not judge one another anymore, but rather determine this – not to put an obstacle or stumbling block in a brother's way" (Romans 14:13).

Cain, the first child born on the earth, offered a sacrifice not pleasing to God. Perversion of worship has continued in the world since that time. Worship must be given to God in the way He has prescribed. He does not accept other ways.

The seriousness of giving acceptable worship to God makes us want to know what attitudes, forms and purposes are acceptable. It also involves knowing the difference between human innovations and what is merely an expedient necessary for doing what God has decreed.

Worship is to God and for God. We were made to worship. The nature of God demands worship. Worship's purpose is not to make people feel better; it is to acknowledge the awesome presence of God in a spirit of humble submission.

Worship enables us to understand more fully our relationship with God. It bridges the gap between Creator and creature. It unites the different natures of spirit and matter. It unites the eternal and the temporal in sweet communion.

Worship is the only thing we can give to God that is our own to give!

QUESTIONS

1. Discuss each of the 11 issues of tension in light of the following criteria:
   - Definitions of worship
   - Scriptural authority
   - Threefold source of worship
   - Threefold purposes of worship

2. Discuss the differences between an expedient for worship and an innovation to worship.

3. What four questions should be asked to determine whether something is an acceptable expedient?

4. How should a Christian regard those who worship a false God?

5. How should a Christian regard those who worship the true God in a false way?

6. Discuss what can be done in a congregation if all do not have the same convictions about worship practices.